Algonquin Provincial Park Management Plan

For further information contact:

Superintendent, Algonquin Provincial Park
P.O. Box 219
Whitney, Ontario
K0J 2M0

Phone: (613) 637–2780
Fax: (613) 637–2864

Drawings by Chris Kerrigan
Photos from the Algonquin Park collection
Design and layout by The HLR Publishing Group, Arnprior, Ont.
Printed by Harpell Printing Ottawa Inc., Ottawa, Ont.

Printed on recycled paper

TITLE: Algonquin Provincial Park Management Plan

MNR 5016
ISBN 0-7778-5273-x

7000 P.R., 1998/September

APPROVAL STATEMENT

It has been 24 years since the first Master Plan was completed for Algonquin Park in 1974. Many things have changed over the years and the various plan Reviews have responded to those changes. The first Park Master Plan Review was completed in 1979; in 1986 a special Review was completed on private cottage leasehold policy; and the most recent Review, in 1989, dealt with an array of more current issues.

In addition, eight separate amendments have been approved to the 1974 Master Plan, dealing with issues from and between reviews. All this activity has resulted in substantive adjustments to a number of policies in the original 1974 plan. Obviously it is time for a new up-to-date plan for the Park to guide day-to-day management and development.

This Plan accomplishes that goal. Indeed, the new plan reflects a fine-tuning of the broad thrust of policies in the 1974 plan that have withstood the test of time. This Plan incorporates a major expansion of the nature reserve and wilderness zone systems and endorses ecosystem sustainability as the first priority of all park and forest management activities. It confirms the commitment to maintain the vast interior of the Park as a backcountry that provides quality 'wilderness' opportunities while peripheral areas look after vehicle-accessible recreation users and their needs. The Plan also recognizes that the needs of society will continue to change and that the Park must evolve and respond to those changing needs within the context of a unique landscape of outstanding natural heritage value to Ontario and the world.

I am pleased to approve the Algonquin Provincial Park Management Plan as the official policy for the management and development of this Park. The Plan reflects this Ministry's intent to protect the natural and cultural features of Algonquin Park, and to maintain and develop high-quality opportunities for backcountry and road-accessible outdoor recreation and heritage appreciation for both residents of Ontario and visitors to the province.

The Management Plan for Algonquin Park will be reviewed regularly throughout its 20-year lifespan to address issues or changing conditions. Significant issues may be dealt with sooner through an amendment process as the need arises. Nevertheless, a mandatory review of the Plan will be held after 10 years.

Norm Richards
Managing Director
Ontario Parks

TABLE OF CONTENTS

LIST OF FIGURES

APPENDICES

Preface

The Algonquin Provincial Park Management Plan

The Algonquin Provincial Park Management Plan replaces the 1974 Algonquin Provincial Park Master Plan as the official plan to guide the development and management of Algonquin Park. The Management Plan includes policies from the 1974 Master Plan, as well as changes introduced as a result of the 1979 and 1989 Plan Reviews, the 1986 Provincial Parks Council Review of Algonquin's Cottage Leaseholder Policy, and previous administrative amendments to the Master Plan (see Section 12.0 for details). The new plan also includes more up-to-date information from reports (earth and life science reports, for example) and other resource documents (such as the Fisheries Management Plan).

The Park Management Plan sets the direction for all other plans developed for the Park (wildlife, forest, and cultural resources management plans, for example). Recognizing the interrelationship of these resources and the Ministry's commitment to sustainability, an ecosystem-based approach, utilizing current scientific knowledge, will be taken in all planning and management activities.

MNR'S Strategic Directions and Statement of Environmental Values

The Ministry of Natural Resources (MNR) is responsible for managing Ontario's natural resources in accordance with the statutes it administers. As the province's lead conservation agency, the Ministry is the steward of provincial parks, natural heritage areas, forests, fisheries, wildlife, aggregates, fuel minerals, and Crown lands and waters that make up 87% of Ontario.

In 1994, the Ministry of Natural Resources finalized its Statement of Environmental Values (SEV) under the Environmental Bill of Rights (EBR). The SEV is a document that describes how the purposes of the EBR are to be considered whenever decisions that might significantly affect the environment are made in the Ministry. During the development of this updated Management Plan, the Ministry has considered its SEV. This Management Plan is intended to reflect the direction sert out in that document and to further the objective of managing our resources on a sustainable basis.

Lands for Life Planning Process and the Role of the Park

In the summer of 1997, the Ministry of Natural Resources commenced the 'Lands for Life' planning process for Crown lands in Ontario. One component of this program — 'Nature's Best Ontario's Parks and Protected Areas: The Framework and Action Plan' — includes the identification of lands and waters for natural heritage protection. Provincial parks currently play and will continue to play a major role in this system.

The role of Algonquin Park within the provincial parks and protected areas system is significant because the Park encompasses two site districts within the Great Lakes-St. Lawrence ecological forest region. An array of provincially significant, representative geological and biological natural heritage values are located within Algonquin Park. Wilderness, Nature Reserve and to a lesser extent Natural Environment zones (approximately 19% of the Park area) ensure the security of these values within the Park so they can contribute to the provincial natural heritage system. The careful management of the intervening park landscape within Recreation/Utilization, Historical, Access and Development zones is critical to the ecological integrity and survival of these landscape values.

In addition, the compatible management of the greater park ecosystem on the public and private land base beyond the Park boundaries is also important to the long-term survival of the representative park ecosystem. The 'Lands for Life' planning program is meant to ensure that this does occur.

1.0 Introduction

Algonquin, the first provincial park in Ontario, protects a variety of natural, cultural, and recreational features and values. As one of the largest provincial parks, Algonquin is biologically diverse with more than 1,000 vascular plant species and more than 200 vertebrates that breed within its boundaries. The Park contains numerous historical and archaeological resources and has inspired more than 40 books, 1,800 scientific papers, a dozen films, a symphony, and the art of Tom Thomson and the Group of Seven. It also provides many opportunities for visitors to appreciate the Park's natural setting while enjoying numerous recreational activities. Accessible from large urban centres and convenient to most tourism travel routes across Ontario, Algonquin Park attracts over half a million visitors yearly who participate in day use activities, camping, or backcountry travel. It occupies 7,630 square kilometres of land and water, with water making up approximately 12% of the area and contributing an extensive network of canoe routes.

Algonquin Park was **established** in 1893 when the Ontario government of the day acted upon a recommendation of the Royal Commission on Forest Reservation and National Parks in "reserving a portion of the ungranted Crown domain to be set apart as a Forest Reservation and National Park." The commissioners envisioned the Park to serve a variety of roles including:

> *maintenance of water supply in a half dozen major water systems, preservation of a primeval forest, protection of birds and animals, a field for experiments in forestry, a place of health resort, and beneficial effects on climate.*

Algonquin Park continues to perform these original functions, and since then has expanded to twice its initial size. The original Park area, consisting of 18 townships (approximately 3797 square kilometres), was designated in 1893 as Algonquin National Park under the *Algonquin National Park Act*. The Park's name was subsequently changed in 1913 to Algonquin Provincial Park, and since 1893 the Park has had its boundaries amended eight times to include 15 additional parcels of land.

Algonquin Park is **located** between Georgian Bay and the Ottawa River in south-central Ontario (**Figure 1**). The Park lies within the area bounded by Highway 11, Highway 62, and the Trans Canada Highway (Highway 17). Highway 60 crosses the southern part of Algonquin over a distance of 63 kilometres. Most Park facilities are concentrated along this corridor.

The Park is surrounded by the communities of Pembroke, North Bay, Huntsville, and Bancroft and a variety of provincial parks, including Samuel de Champlain, Restoule, Mikisew, Arrowhead, Bonnechere, and Driftwood. Four Waterway Provincial Parks border Algonquin with their headwaters protected within the Park: Bonnechere, Upper Madawaska, Opeongo, and Oxtongue Rivers.

Algonquin Provincial Park is situated on the flanks and summit of a dome of Precambrian **Canadian Shield** bedrock with elevations reaching 587 metres above sea level on the west side to 150 metres on the east side of the Park. Five major rivers drain the Park: the Oxtongue, Petawawa, Barron, Madawaska, and Bonnechere.

The Park's topography and geography create variations in the climate and ecosystems. Since it is situated on a dome, the Park has a colder and wetter **climate** compared to surrounding areas. Within the Park, higher elevations on the west side in combination with westerly winds create a wetter, cooler environment on the west side and a dryer, warmer climate on the east side. The Park is also located in a transition zone between the northern boreal forests and southern deciduous hardwood forests, which results in a rich diversity of northern and southern life forms.

Overall, the Park's geographic position and its changes in elevation create variations in climate, soils and aquatic conditions, which consequently affect the plant and animal life.

According to the Ministry's ecological land classification system, where areas are classified on the basis of their climate and landform relationships, the Park is situated in the Georgian Bay Site Region (5E) (**Figure 2**). This region is an area of rolling uplands and bedrock outcrops with areas of sand and gravel of glacial origin. The region sustains primarily Sugar Maple (*Acer saccharum*), Yellow Birch (*Betula alleghaniensis*), Hemlock (*Tsuga canadensis*), and White Pine (*Pinus strobus*) on the upland sites while Black Spruce (*Picea mariana*) dominates the lowland sites.

Within the Georgian Bay Site Region, the Park is part of two site districts, each with distinctive physiographic and biotic conditions. The west side of the Park is part of the Algonquin Park Site District (5E-9) while the east side comprises about half of the Brent Site District (5E-10). Differences in soils combine with the differences in topography and climate to create different forests on the west and east sides. On the west side in Site District 5E-9, the soils are primarily glacial tills and the land is relatively high and rugged, creating a wetter and cooler climate. As a result, mature climax forests of tolerant hardwoods such as Sugar Maple, Yellow Birch, and American Beech (*Fagus grandifolia*) exist interspersed with softwoods species such as Hemlock and White Pine.

On the east side of the Park, in Site District 5E-10, the soil is post-glacial outwash and the climate is drier and warmer since the landscape is lower and the hills more gently rolling. Here, the forest has been influenced by drier soil and a higher incidence of fire. Forest growth is a mixture of Trembling Aspen (*Populus tremuloides*), White Birch (*Betula papyrifera*), White Pine, Red Pine (*Pinus resinosa*), and Red Maple (*Acer rubrum*). Black Spruce, Tamarack (*Larix laricina*), Eastern White Cedar (*Thuja occidentalis*), and Balsam Fir (*Abies balsamea*) dominate the lowland areas throughout the Park.

Algonquin Park's **earth science** features include glaciofluvial landforms formed by meltwater channels during past glacial drainage. The Park is a provincially significant example of a landscape typifying an ice stagnation environment and displays such surficial features as eskers, kettles, kame moraines, terraces, drumlins, deltas, outwash plains, sand dunes, beach ridges, meltwater channels, and boulder deposits. The Park also contains the largest kame-moraine complex in the region and significant geological features such as a fault canyon (Barron Canyon) and a meteorite crater (Brent Crater). In addition, the existence of such features as striations, crescentic scars, drumlins and former meltwater channels reveals the history of glacial Lake Wisconsin ice flow and the Upper Great Lakes drainage in the region. Significant representation of the region's bedrock, part of the Precambrian Grenville Province, is also evident.

Barron Canyon

Algonquin Park contains a diverse and rich assemblage of **life science features**. There are variations of lowland/upland, tolerant/intolerant, and coniferous or deciduous forest types, as well as wetland complexes and entire watershed units. The Park also contains areas of natural disturbance such as former burns or blowdowns. In addition, many uncommon species have been identified in the Park, including the nationally rare Purple Cliffbrake (*Pellaea atropurpurea*) and Southern Twayblade (*Listera australis*), as well as provincially rare species such as White-fringed Orchid (*Platanthera blephariglottis*), Triangle Grapefern (*Botrychium lanceolatum*), and Flat Poverty Grass (*Danthonia compressa*).

Wildlife communities are diverse. Moose (*Alces alces*), White-tailed Deer (*Odocoileus virginianus*), Timber Wolf (*Canis lupus*), River Otter (*Lutra canadensis*), and American Black Bear (*Ursus americanus*) are some of the larger mammals. The Park supports more than 100 species of breeding birds, including such northern species as the Boreal Chickadee (*Parus hudsonicus*) and the Gray Jay (*Perisoreus canadensis*), not often encountered at the lower elevations surrounding the Park.

Provincially significant wildlife species include the Red-shouldered Hawk (*Buteo lineatus*) and the provincially vulnerable Wood Turtle (*Clemmys insculpta*). Algonquin Park also contains the only major complex of relatively intact native trout fisheries remaining in southern Ontario. These fisheries provide an exceptionally high quality angling experience.

Extensive field research has identified an impressive array of **historic and archaeological sites**, including former ranger cabins, camboose camps, old railway lines, and pictograph sites. Algonquin Park's waterways are also historically important as they served as early travel routes.

The Park's **resources** have played an important role in the establishment and continued viability of surrounding communities. At the time of the Park's creation in 1893, parts of it had already been logged for nearly 60 years to meet the demands of the Ottawa Valley timber trade. Today, most of Algonquin Park consists of forest that averages 80 to 100 years of age and continues to support the forest industry through sustainable forest management practices. Primary forest products manufacturing and tourism provide employment for residents of the region. Consequently, the continued productivity of the resource base in the Park is important to this region's economy and to the livelihood of communities surrounding the Park.

Over the years, **policies** have been developed for Algonquin Park's long-term protection, development, and management (see Section 12.0). The policies contained in this consolidated management plan will continue to guide park managers in integrating resource and recreational uses in Algonquin while protecting the Park's natural qualities.

The matters set out in this document are without prejudice to, and may be superseded by, any settlements of claims made between the Ontario Government and First Nations in Ontario.

Figure 1 — Provincial Context

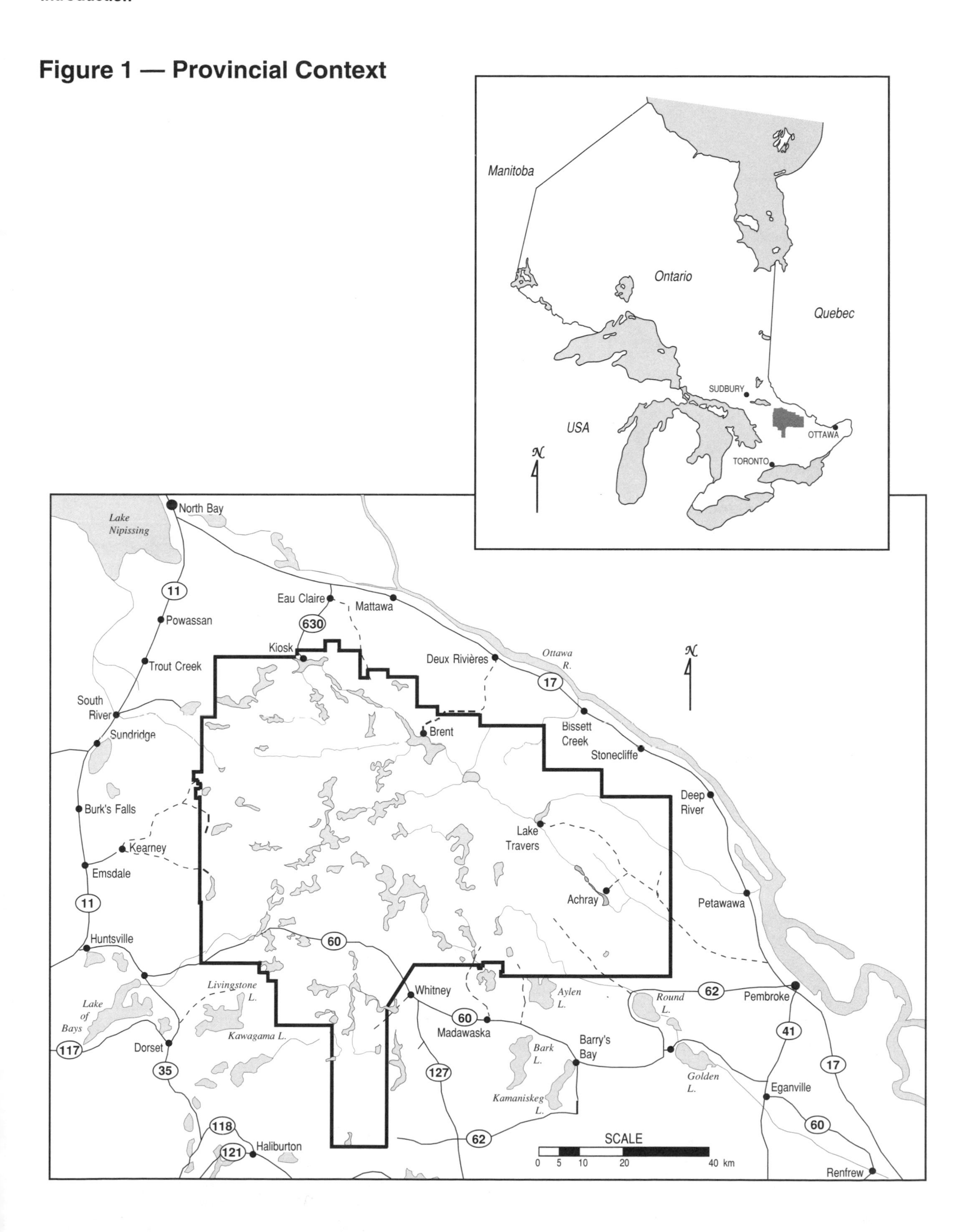

Figure 2 — Site Regions and Districts

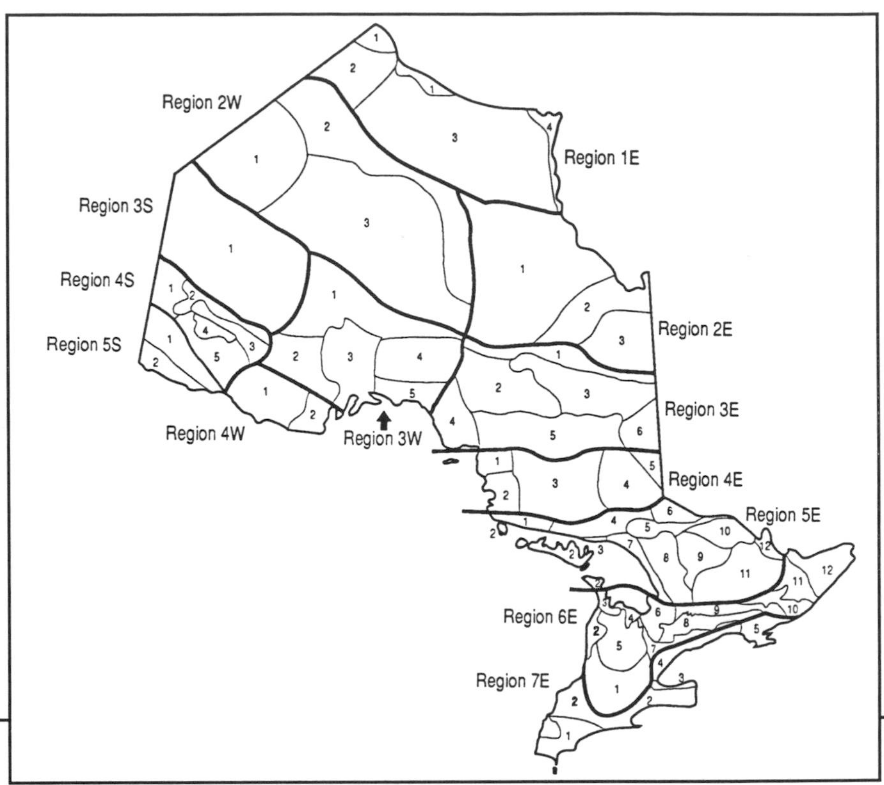

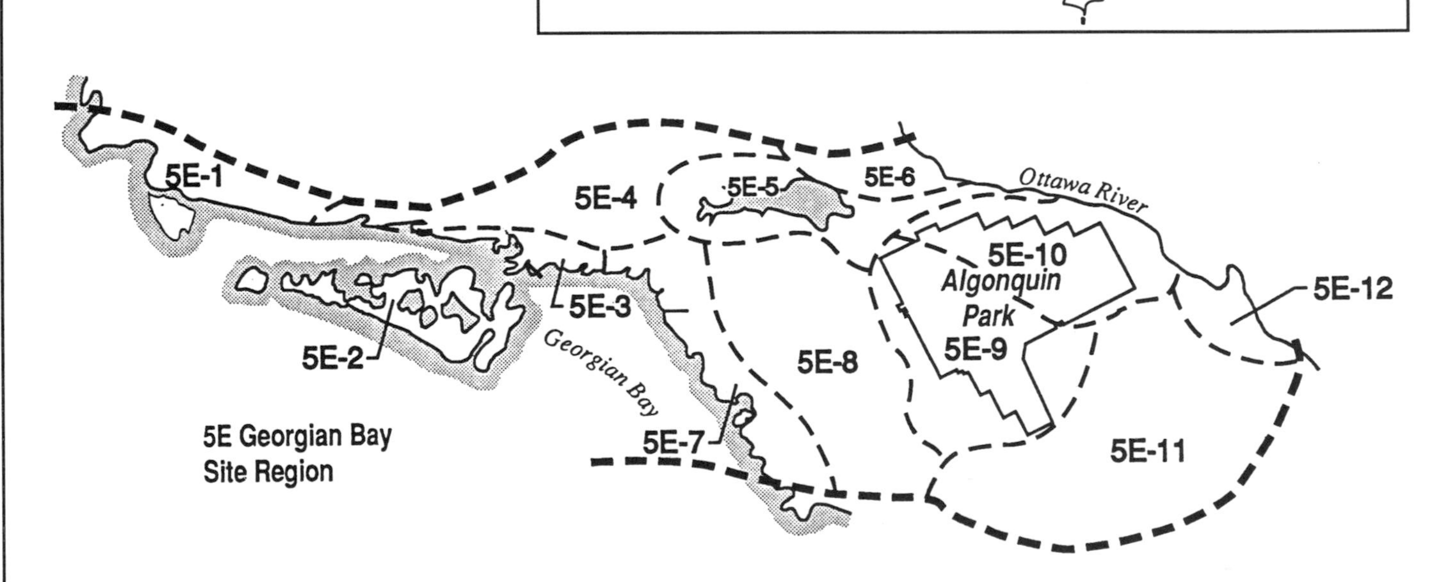

2.0 Classification

Algonquin Provincial Park is a **Natural Environment Park** and has been planned, zoned, and managed in accordance with the policies for this class of park:

> *Natural Environment Parks incorporate outstanding recreational landscapes with representative natural features and historical resources to provide high-quality recreational and educational experiences.*

Algonquin Provincial Park has been classified as a Natural Environment Park in recognition of its outstanding recreational environment and abundance of natural and cultural resources. Algonquin's recreational opportunities are numerous, ranging from semi-wilderness experiences such as backpacking, snowshoeing, canoeing, and camping in the Interior of the Park to picnicking, swimming, hiking, cross-country skiing, and camping in the more developed areas. In addition, Algonquin's scenery and wildlife attract many visitors. Algonquin also has tremendous scientific value, containing significant earth and life science features as well as historical and archaeological sites.

White Pine

3.0 Goal

Algonquin Park contributes to the provincial parks system by protecting such values as plant communities, wildlife, and cultural resources while providing a variety of recreational opportunities. Algonquin also serves to maintain the economic base of many local communities and will continue to contribute to resource production in the region.

In accordance with its classification, the goal of Algonquin Provincial Park is:

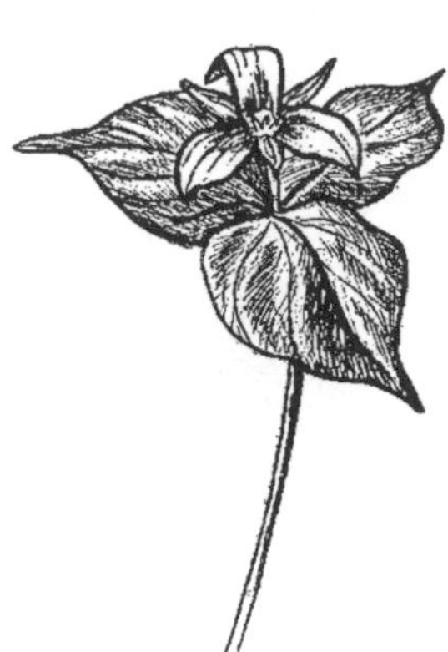

> *To provide protection of natural and cultural features, continuing opportunities for a diversity of low-intensity recreational, wilderness, and natural environmental experiences; and within this provision continue and enhance the Park's contribution to the economic, social, and cultural life of the region.*

Algonquin Park contributes to the goal of the provincial parks system, which is:

> *To provide a variety of outdoor recreation opportunities and to protect provincially significant natural, cultural, and recreational environments in a system of provincial parks.*

The Park also advances the Ministry of Natural Resources' goal:

> *To contribute to the environmental, social, and economic well-being of Ontario through the sustainable development of natural resources.*

Hemlock

4.0 Objectives

To fulfil its goal, Algonquin Park has five objectives. The Park contributes to the four provincial parks system objectives of protection, recreation, heritage appreciation, and tourism. Algonquin's role in resource utilization also generates a fifth objective — resource management.

4.1 Protection Objective

To protect provincially significant elements of the natural and cultural landscape of Algonquin Park.

The Park's location in the transition zone between the northern boreal and the southern deciduous hardwood forests, as well as its topographic variations, provides a rich diversity of flora and fauna, including some regionally and provincially significant communities and species. Algonquin Park also contains a variety of earth science features representing post-glacial features. Nature Reserve Zones (see Section 6.1) have been designated within the Park to provide protection for these significant or representative earth and life science features. Wilderness Zones have been designated to protect significant natural and cultural features and to protect areas providing wilderness recreational experiences. The Park also protects a variety of historic and archaeological sites within Historical Zones (see Sections 6.2 and 8.6) for educational and research purposes.

Additional inventories and further research will be encouraged to improve our knowledge of the Park's environments and to establish scientific benchmark areas preserving Algonquin's representative and significant features.

Fox

Provincial parks are key contributors to Ontario's protected areas. Along with national parks, conservation reserves, conservation authority lands, and other areas, they help to protect our natural and cultural heritage.

Algonquin contributes to the protection of the ecological integrity and diversity of the province in two ways. It protects significant environments and features within the Park boundary. It is also a core area in the regional natural heritage system, as many of the values or ecological processes for which the Park was set aside extend beyond its borders.

The protection of Park values is therefore partly dependent on appropriate environmental management outside the Park. In turn, the Park provides a scientific and management benchmark that can be used for comparison purposes to help measure ecological integrity in the greater Park ecosystem.

4.2 Recreation Objective

To provide outdoor recreation opportunities ranging from high-intensity day use to low-intensity wilderness experiences.

Algonquin Provincial Park offers a wide range of all-season activities, from back-country travel and camping in the Interior of the Park to car camping and day use in the more developed areas. All programs and publications associated with recreational activities emphasize the Park's protection objective and encourage heritage appreciation.

The recreation capacity of the Park is established for various activities to ensure ecosystem sustainability, minimize environmental damage, reduce conflicts between users, and for safety purposes. Current levels of traditional, water-oriented summer uses, such as car camping along the Highway 60 Parkway Corridor and canoe tripping in the Interior, are close to the Park's capacity. Expansion of recreational use will be directed to other seasons and to other areas of the Park for activities such as horseback riding, mountain biking, snowshoeing, and dogsledding.

Interior management is aimed at preserving and maintaining the Algonquin Interior "wilderness" experience. Current uses include canoe tripping, backpacking, cross-country skiing, snowshoeing, and dogsledding. Canoe camping is close to capacity, and the total number of sites will be maintained at or close to current levels. The backpacking trails are meeting current demand, but opportunities

Winter camp

may increase with the development of new backpacking trails, if required. There is additional potential for cross-country skiing, snowshoeing, dogsledding, and associated winter camping.

On the direction of the 1989 Review, the Park has looked into modest roofed accommodation alternatives. Existing historical ranger cabins are being made available to Interior users through the reservation system. The potential also exists for roofed accommodation at Lake Travers and Cedar Lake. Only existing buildings will be considered for use in the Interior. Any new cabins or roofed accommodation would be near areas of existing public access.

Interior visitors also participate in other seasonal activities such as swimming, sunbathing, scenic/wildlife viewing, and fishing. Hunting and seasonal hunt camps are permitted in Clyde, Bruton, and Eyre (McRae Addition) Townships.

Car campgrounds, including a group campground, are located along the Parkway Corridor and in some peripheral areas of the Park. Car campsites in the corridor will be maintained at or close to current levels, and future development and upgrading of campgrounds will occur primarily in the peripheral areas.

Commercial lodges and **youth camps**, which are privately operated, provide accommodation and enable guests to enjoy day use activities in the Park.

Day use facilities and services have been developed that provide opportunities for swimming, picnicking, biking, cross-country skiing, and heritage appreciation on interpretive trails. Additional day use opportunities for mountain biking, hiking, cross-country skiing, and new opportunities for horseback riding and dogsledding may be provided.

Visitors also participate in such day use activities as walking, scenic/wildlife viewing, snowshoeing, fishing, snowmobiling, and day hunting in Clyde, Bruton, and Eyre Townships.

No new interior **access points** will be developed except for the consideration of a southern entry in the Galipo Lakes area.

4.3 Heritage Appreciation Objective

To provide opportunities for exploration and appreciation of the outdoor natural and cultural heritage of Algonquin Park.

Algonquin Park's natural beauty and rich history provide many opportunities for visitors to appreciate the heritage of the Park. The Park's interpretive program (a component of the Natural Heritage Education Program) uses facilities such as the Visitor Centre, the Logging Museum, interpretive trails, illustrated talks, staff-led activities and publications to encourage an appreciation for the Park's natural and historic values. Almost one million contacts are made annually through the Natural Heritage Education Program in an effort to orient visitors to Algonquin's special qualities and provide them with an opportunity to gain a deeper understanding of the natural, educational, scientific, and historical aspects of the Park.

4.4 Tourism Objective

To provide Ontario's residents and out-of-province visitors with opportunities to discover and experience the distinctive regions of Algonquin Park.

Algonquin Park's natural beauty, abundant wildlife, and recreational opportunities continue to attract tourists from across Ontario and the world. The marketing and tourism strategy for Algonquin Park will continue to target specific visitor and user groups and provide them with opportunities to experience the attractions of Algonquin. This will involve communicating and working with tourist organizations.

4.5 Resource Management Objective

To practise sustainable resource management in Algonquin Park for the long-term health of the Park's ecosystems and to provide recreational, cultural, and economic benefits.

The protection of the Park's significant natural, cultural, and recreational values is paramount. Within this parameter the renewable resources of Algonquin Park are and will continue to be managed on a sustainable basis. Management plans have been or will be prepared for all resource uses in the Park to ensure that the Park's resources are managed in this manner.

Forest management activities are permitted in the Recreation/Utilization Zone. Algonquin Park is an anomaly in the parks system as this is the only provincial park where these activities occur.

The Algonquin Park Forest Management Plan describes silvicultural practices (including harvesting and renewal activities) that are designed to protect Park values such as wildlife, fisheries, tourism, and outdoor recreation. All forest management activities must be in accordance with the Park Management Plan.

For the purposes of forest management operations and minor Park maintenance projects, aggregate resource extraction is permitted in the Recreation/Utilization Zone of the Park in accordance with provincial guidelines and policies.

Trapping has been permitted on registered traplines in the Recreation/Utilization Zone of Clyde and Bruton Townships since those townships were added to the Park in 1961. Since 1958, the Algonquins of Ontario have held trapping licences on 19 registered traplines in the eastern and central parts of the Park.

Public hunting and hunt camps have been permitted in the Recreation/Utilization Zone in Clyde and Bruton Townships since they were added to the Park in 1961. Public hunting also occurs in part of Eyre Township (the McRae Addition), which was added to the Park in 1993.

Hunting is carried out by the Algonquins of Ontario in the east half of the Park under the provisions of the "Algonquin Hunting Agreement." The provisions cover such matters as hunting areas, species, harvest numbers, sex/age ratios, monitoring, enforcement, and reporting of harvest. An agreement has been negotiated each year since 1991, pending the outcome of negotiations of the Algonquins' of Ontario land claim.

Fishing is also permitted in most areas. Hunting, trapping, and fishing are managed to maintain a sustainable resource base while providing recreational or economic opportunities.

4.6 Guiding Principles

In addition to a goal and objectives, there is also a set of nine principles that is used to guide the management of the provincial parks **system**. The principles are included below with a description of how they relate to Algonquin.

Permanence

The provincial parks system is dedicated for all time to the present and future generations of the people of Ontario for their healthful enjoyment and appreciation.

Algonquin was Ontario's first provincial park. Since 1893 it has protected significant earth and life science, historical archaeological, and recreational resources — and will continue to do so for future generations.

Distinctiveness

Provincial parks provide a distinctive range of quality outdoor recreation experiences, many of which cannot be provided in other types of parks, for example, wilderness travel and appreciation.

Algonquin is renowned for its high-quality outdoor day use, car camping, and back-country travel opportunities unique in southern Ontario. Algonquin is among a select group of parks that is capable of providing a wide range of recreation experiences.

Representation

Provincial parks are established to secure for posterity representative features of Ontario's natural and cultural heritage. Wherever possible, the best representations of our heritage will be included in the parks system.

Algonquin Park, at the southern end of the Canadian Shield, contains earth science, life science, and cultural features and environments that provide excellent examples of the diverse heritage of this part of Ontario.

Variety

The provincial parks system provides a wide variety of outdoor recreation opportunities, and protected natural and cultural landscapes and features.

By virtue of its size and diversity, Algonquin Park has one of the widest variety of recreation opportunities and protected areas located in any single park in the system.

Accessibility

The benefits of the system will be distributed as widely as possible geographically and as equitably as possible socially so that they are accessible to all Ontario residents.

Algonquin's many features and facilities are located close to the main population centres of Ontario. Provincial parks strive to provide a range of facilities and services that are affordable and that will serve visitors of varying physical abilities.

Coordination

The provincial parks system will be managed to complement, rather than compete with, the private sector and other public agencies.

Algonquin's protected environments contribute to private, provincial, and federal efforts to safeguard samples of the natural and cultural heritage of Ontario and of Canada. Algonquin encourages and relies on the contribution of the private sector to provide support for its visitors and its operations. The Park is a world-renowned attraction and plays a significant role in regional tourism.

System

Individual provincial parks contribute to the overall objectives of the provincial parks system; all objectives may not be met in each park. The parks system, rather than the individual parks, provides the diversity of experiences and landscapes that are sought.

As with all other provincial parks, Algonquin contributes to the diversity of experiences and landscapes in the province-wide system. While its contributions to resource protection and the provision of recreation opportunities are very significant, the Park is also part of a larger network of protected areas in the province.

Classification

No individual park can be all things to all people. Park classification organizes Ontario's provincial parks into broad categories, each of which has particular purposes and characteristics as well as distinctive planning, management, and visitor services (Natural Heritage Education) policies.

Algonquin is classified as a Natural Environment Park. The other classifications are Wilderness, Nature Reserve, Historical, Waterway and Recreation Parks. Natural Environment Parks provide a balance of resource protection and outdoor recreation.

Zoning

Ontario's provincial parks are zoned on the basis of resource significance and recreation potential; various types of zones ensure that users get the most out of individual parks. Planning and management policies appropriate to each zone type are applied consistently throughout the parks system.

Each of the six park classes may contain a variety of zones, although only two classes — natural environment and waterway — may include all six zone types (i.e. nature reserve, wilderness, natural environment, historical, development and access). Algonquin contains all six, as well as a seventh that is unique to it — a Recreation/Utilization Zone, where forest management activities occur.

5.0 Park Land

Algonquin Provincial Park covers an area of 7630 square kilometres, most of it being in the District of Nipissing and part in the northeast corner of Haliburton County. The official boundaries of the Park are described in O.Reg. 386/93 made under the *Provincial Parks Act*. The purpose of O.Reg. 386/93 was to amend the boundary description of Algonquin Provincial Park (as previously defined in Reg. 951, R.R.O. 1990, designation of parks).

5.1 Additions

Two areas of Crown land will be considered for inclusion in Algonquin Park. Once added, both areas will be zoned Recreation/Utilization and will be subject to the policies of that zone type.

- **Tim River**: An area of approximately 80 hectares on the west side may be added to the Park. It encloses the section of the Tim River located between the existing boundary of the Park and the Tim River access point. The purpose of extending the boundary is to include the access point and more of the river's headwaters in the Park.
- **Brain Lake**: On the north side of the Park, a 400-hectare parcel of Crown land just west of Brain Lake may be included since it is already bounded by the Park on three sides.

5.2 Land Occupation/Tenure

The boundary of Algonquin Park encloses public lands but also includes private land, rights-of-way, land use permits, licences of occupation, federally administered lands, and private and commercial leases.

- The Park will be retained in public ownership, and land uses that may adversely affect its qualities and character will be prohibited.
- All alienated lands within the Park will be acquired by 2017 and made available for public purposes.
- Removal of structures and site restoration should occur as quickly as possible after expiration of the covering lease, special use permit or upon acquisition of private land.
- The policy of removal will not apply to buildings that should be retained for Park use because of their historical significance.

There are a total of 511 hectares of alienated land in the Park.

- Approximately 8 hectares of private land, in small parcels, contain privately owned cottage lots situated on Madawaska, Whitefish, Cauliflower, Kingscote and Kioshkokwi Lakes. These properties are to be acquired by the year 2017.
- The remaining 503 hectares are **Canadian National Railway** (CNR) lands used for its railway right-of-way and station grounds. CNR is going through the abandonment process for this line. When the Crown acquires this right-of-way, it will be added to Algonquin Park.

The **Algonquin Radio Observatory** is federally administered. Located on 54 hectares of land near Lake Travers, the research facilities are administered by Natural Resources Canada under the *National Radio Observatory Act 1962-3*. Under this legislation, the control and management of the land are retained by the Ontario Ministry of Natural Resources.

- Upon cessation of operations by the Algonquin Radio Observatory, all existing facilities will be removed and the site will be rehabilitated.

There are 305 cottage properties held under lease, licence, or land use permit in the Park (as of January 1998).

- All cottage leases will be terminated on or before December 31, 2017.
- There is no provision for renewal.
- The Park Superintendent is required to ensure that all lessees comply with the terms of their leases, particularly in obtaining authorization from the Superintendent for any construction, clearing or shoreline work.
- All cottage lot development is controlled by the *Construction and Development Standards: Algonquin Park Cottage Leaseholds* (Appendix A).
- The standards may be revised to address new environmental concerns or development restrictions.

There are 65 *temporary* **hunting camp sites**, authorized by special **permits** (under Regulation 501, *Game and Fish Act*, RSO 1990), that are used during the fall hunting season in Clyde and Bruton Townships. And, in the McRae Addition (Eyre Township), there are two *permanent* recreational camps under land use permits and 14 *temporary* hunt camps.

- These uses will be permitted to continue as long as hunting is permitted within these areas of the Park.

Land use permits and **licences of occupation** are used for utilities in the Park. The Ontario Hydro transmission lines and Bell Canada telephone facilities exist under land use permits and a licence of occupation, respectively. Ontario Hydro occupies 1335 hectares of land under a land use permit for its transmission line and distribution lines. Bell Canada uses the existing right-of-way for its utility lines and has a licence of occupation for its switching station along Highway 60.

- The Park Superintendent will approve the location and development of all new structures associated with these land authorizations and of all new telephone and hydro distribution lines. These will be underground whenever possible.
- No new hydro transmission lines such as the Minden-Des Joachims transmission line will be built in or through the Park.
- The Minden-Des Joachims line right-of-way will not be widened.
- Following the cessation of operations, all facilities associated with the land authorizations will be removed by the respective organization.

There are nine **commercial leases** in the Park. These private-sector enterprises include three lodges and six youth camps.

The lodges provide accommodation and services to a segment of society that does not choose to camp yet wishes to experience the natural environment of the Park. Indeed, the lodges encourage their patrons to partake of the various Park programs as they are available. Existing commercial lodges have leases that expired on December 31, 1996, with a further right of renewal for a 21-year-period, plus a further right of renewal for a period of time that has yet to be determined.

The youth camps make a substantial contribution by making young people aware of natural areas like Algonquin Park. Youth camps will be encouraged to pursue programs that foster an understanding and appreciation of the natural environment. The development of new or the renovation of existing facilities to accommodate young people and provide educational programs may also be considered in the Park. Existing youth camp leases also expired in 1996 and they provided for a renewal term of 21 years plus a further right of renewal dependent on prevailing government policy at that time.

- Ontario Parks recognizes the contributions that both youth camps and lodges make to Algonquin and commenced to negotiate lease renewals in 1997.
- All commercial leaseholders will follow the *Construction and Development Standards: Algonquin Park Commercial Leaseholds* (Appendix B), which are similar to the non-commercial leases in the Park.

Opeongo Store

5.3 The Park Perimeter

The use of lands surrounding Algonquin is of concern to the Park. Therefore, management and development proposals outside the Park boundary that may affect the Park's natural, cultural, and recreational values will be reviewed by the Park Superintendent. Land use activities will not be unduly restricted. Rather, resource management activities will be encouraged to take place in a manner that does not have a negative impact on Park values. Proposals will be reviewed through the Ministry's land use planning process to identify areas of concern (see *Guidelines for Resource Management and Land Use Activities along the Perimeter of Algonquin Park*, Appendix C).

Existing land uses around Algonquin are also monitored by Ministry staff. For example, the Bracebridge Area Office reviews the plans and monitors the operation of the graphite mine adjacent to the Park in Butt Township and advises Park management staff on issues of relevance to the Park.

6.0 Zoning

Zoning is essential to the orderly development and effective management of a park. Areas within Algonquin Park are zoned to allocate their resource values to their most appropriate use in a natural environment park. Zoning is based on an area's significance for protection and potential for recreational and resource uses. Natural environment parks always include Natural Environment and Development Zones and may also include Nature Reserve, Wilderness, Historical and Access Zones.

Algonquin Provincial Park zoning includes all six zones and an additional zone unique to Algonquin — the Recreation/Utilization Zone (**Figure 3**) — that permits forest management activities. The list below illustrates the amount of Park area (land and water) in each zone type.

Zone Type	Area (ha.)	% of Park area
Nature Reserve	39,250	5.1
Wilderness	90,475	11.9
Natural Environment	13,765	1.8
Historical	1,680	0.2
Development	22,545	3.0
Access	735	0.1
Recreation/Utilization	594,860	77.9
Total	763,310	100.0

6.1 Nature Reserve Zones

Nature Reserve Zones include any significant earth and life science features that require management distinct from that in adjacent zones.

Algonquin Park's Nature Reserve Zone system delineates and protects representative and significant earth and life science features. These may include relatively undisturbed examples of typical habitat types, landform features, complexes or phenomena, as well as rare biogeographically important and/or exceptional populations of floral and faunal species. In total, 88 Nature Reserve Zones have been designated in the Park ranging in size from a few hectares to more than 5,200 hectares and covering a total area of 39,250 hectares or 5.1% of the Park area. (See Appendix D)

Provincial Park Planning and Management Policies (1993) do not permit campsite development within Nature Reserve Zones. However, interior camping is an existing use in some Nature Reserve Zones. Since overnight trails and canoe routes have been permitted within these zones, campsites are required. Therefore, interior campsites will continue to be permitted in Nature Reserve Zones provided they will not impair the natural values within these zones. These facilities (campsites, portages, trails and signs for route identification) will be provided where required and will be recognized as non-conforming uses within these zones. Temporary facilities for management or approved research may also be permitted where appropriate.

6.1.1 Natural Heritage Value Identification and Protection

Two science concepts are used to describe natural diversity and identify a system of natural heritage areas for protection in Ontario — representation and special values. Representation is the primary concept and identifies areas that are the best examples of natural diversity through features, species and ecosystems. The second concept identifies special values, like endangered species' habitat, which may or may not be representative but are still significant.

Representative natural diversity is defined through three complementary processes — geological, terrestrial and aquatic. Geological (earth science) diversity is defined by distinct and enduring features on the landscape created by processes that can be distinguished by their age, stratigraphy and topography. Representative features are organized into 44 themes, rock types, fossil assemblages, landforms and related geological processes. These features are the foundation upon which biodiversity (terrestrial and aquatic) flourishes.

Terrestrial (life science) diversity is defined on the basis of 14 site regions and their component 69 site districts. Site regions are broad geoclimatic zones distinguished by temperature and precipitation gradients. A site district is a distinctive physiographic area found within a site region, containing landform patterns and biological productivity traits that distinguish it from other site districts. Within a site district, smaller landscape units are defined based on

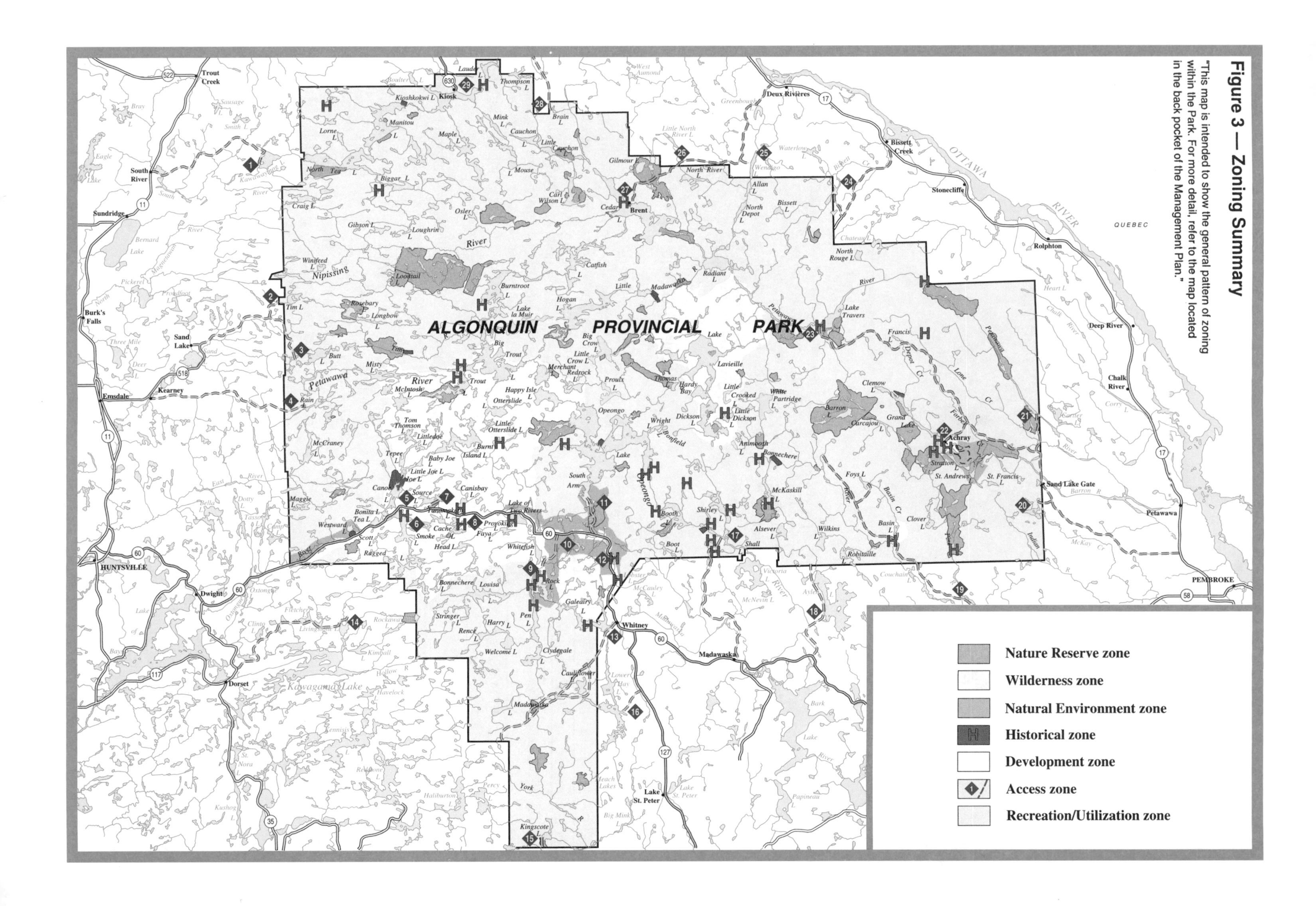

Figure 3 — Zoning Summary
"This map is intended to show the general pattern of zoning within the Park. For more detail, refer to the map located in the back pocket of the Management Plan."
ALGONQUIN PROVINCIAL PARK
OTTAWA RIVER
QUEBEC
PEMBROKE
Petawawa
Chalk River
Deep River
Rolphton
Stonecliffe
Bissett Creek
Deux Rivières
Sand Lake Gate
Whitney
Madawaska
Lake St. Peter
Dorset
Dwight
HUNTSVILLE
Emsdale
Kearney
Sand Lake
Burk's Falls
Sundridge
South River
Trout Creek
Kiosk
Brent
Achray
Kawagama Lake
Nature Reserve zone
Wilderness zone
Natural Environment zone
Historical zone
Development zone
Access zone
Recreation/Utilization zone

re-occurring landform patterns. These patterns and the vegetation communities and species they support constitute the values to be represented.

At present, aquatic (life science) diversity is only partially defined through wetland classification and lake/stream descriptions (e.g., warm and cold water), and is generally represented through the two previous approaches.

Special values are defined on the basis of species, features and ecosystems: uniqueness, rarity, sensitivity or the specific value placed on them by society. Specific criteria exist to determine significance (e.g., wetlands, old growth and endangered species). Provincially significant special values are included within the natural heritage areas system.

Once all of these provincially significant values have been identified, the next step is to determine the most effective means of protecting them into the future. **Provincial parks** are one of the principal (highest order) designations for the protection of natural heritage values, be they representative or special. Indeed, one of the primary roles of provincial parks is to protect the best natural values within their boundaries before considering the accommodation of other park objectives. Nature Reserve Zones are one of the primary means of protecting the best representative and/or special natural heritage values within a park landscape.

Algonquin Park contains both earth and life science values within its system of Nature Reserve Zones. The system of earth science Nature Reserve Zones includes individual structural and surficial features or landscape formations designated provincially significant because of their relationship to glacial Lake Algonquin. Because the Park is situated in two site districts (5E-9/10) within site region 5E, it contains an array of provincially significant life science values and features (**Figure 2**). Twenty-seven of the 88 Nature Reserve Zones in the Park include significant earth science values and 76 zones contain significant life science values, with a number of zones containing both values. Some of these values are described below.

6.1.2 Earth Science

Algonquin Park protects both significant and representative earth science features in Nature Reserve Zones. These zones protect both bedrock and surficial features of earth science value.

Algonquin Park is located on part of the Canadian Precambrian Shield known as the Grenville Province. It is further differentiated into distinct areas of **bedrock** called "terranes" and "domains." Each of these divisions is characterized by a distinctive assemblage of rock types, structural features (e.g., type or degree of folding), and grades of metamorphism (alteration due to the effect of pressure and/or heat). The Park provides excellent representation of the Kiosk, McCraney, McClintock, Powassan, and Opeongo domains within the Algonquin terrane. There is also good representation of the Central Metasedimentary Belt, a zone of extreme shearing in the southern part of the Park.

The bedrock geology of Algonquin Park is of Middle to Late Precambrian age (1800 to 1400 million years old). The predominant rock formations are pink to grey-banded quartz-feldspar-biotite orthogneiss and metasediments, which have been intruded by a variety of granitic and mafic rocks. These rocks were subjected to metamorphism during a mountain-building period (the Grenville Orogeny), which culminated approximately 1000 million years ago. As a result, the rocks were recrystallized and deformed into folded gneiss. Granitic pegmatite and mafic dikes were intruded later. This tectonic activity produced the domains in the Park and the series of faults (part of the Ottawa Valley-Bonnechere Graben System) on the east side of the Park. By about 600 million years ago, the rocks were reduced by erosion to their present level. On this surface, sediments were laid down in warm seas during Ordovician and Silurian time. Limestones and clastic sedimentary rocks were almost completely removed in the Park area by the subsequent 400 million years of erosion, including the glacial erosion of the last two million years.

Barron Canyon

The Nature Reserve Zone system identifies some significant geological features such as sections of the Ottawa Bonnechere Graben along the Barron Canyon and Petawawa River. The Brent Crater has also been protected in a Nature Reserve Zone. The Brent Crater is a circular depression located on the northern boundary of Algonquin Park in Deacon and Cameron Townships. The Crater was formed between 1000 and 450 million years ago (prior to the Ordovician) and has been described as a crater of cryptovolcanic origin or, more likely, a meteorite impact crater. The Brent Crater depression has preserved a bed of Ordovician limestone, a vestige of the blanket of limestone that once covered Algonquin Park. The bedrock geology of the Park requires detailed study to identify significant interpretive localities. These may be protected in future Nature Reserve Zones, most of very small extent.

Within the Park, significant **surficial** earth science features provide important information about the glacial history of the Park, including the drainage of glacial Lake Algonquin. The Park landscape represents an ancient erosional surface 2.5 to 1.0 million years old (Early to Middle Proterozoic age). The Park's rugged Precambrian bedrock was eroded by ice and meltwater during several periods of glaciation. However, there is only evidence of the last glaciation, which took place during the Late Wisconsinan period. Much of the Park remained covered in ice from about 80,000 years ago up until about 12,000 years ago.

The highland topography resulted in stagnation of the melting ice, which produced widespread ice-contact sedimentation and stratified drift over much of the Park. Since ice stagnation was a relatively uncommon phenomenon in areas of the province affected by large glacial lakes, the Park provides a provincially significant example of this type of landscape. As a result, glacial deposits including glacial tills, ice-contact stratified drift, and glaciofluvial deposits are well represented in Algonquin Park.

Glacial till deposits are widespread and occur as a variety of features, including ground moraine, drumlins, drumlinoid and crag and tail features, morainic ridges and end moraines. Moraines are of particular interest as they provide location data for former positions of the ice front. The provincially significant DeGeer-type moraines found on the southeast side of Lake Travers were formed while the melting ice was in contact with a proglacial lake. These small parallel ridges formed at the base of the ice and may represent annual fluctuations in the ice front. Other significant ice positions are marked by a large moraine in Fitzgerald Township and morainic ridges near Hailstorm Creek.

Ice-contact stratified drift deposits form a suite of distinctive landforms, including kames, eskers and kame terraces. These deposits, which are formed on or adjacent to melting ice, develop faults, slumps, and other internal deformation features as the supporting glacial ice melts away. The kame terraces found along the Little Madawaska River west of Radiant Lake are considered provincially significant as their form characterizes alpine glaciation rather than continental glaciation, which typically affected the Park. Major esker complexes have been identified along the Crow River east of White Partridge Lake.

Deposits from glacial meltwater had a significant impact on Algonquin Park's east side. The Petawawa, Barron, Indian and Bonnechere Rivers, and Forbes Creek all served as meltwater channels during the drainage of glacial Lake Algonquin to the Champlain Sea east of the Park. It is believed that the first outlet for this drainage occurred through White Partridge Lake, Robitaille Creek and the Bonnechere River valley. A proglacial lake associated with the White Partridge Lake outlet may have been a major arm of Lake Algonquin. Large volumes of water likely cut the provincially significant terraces found south of White Partridge Lake. Other depositional features relating to these flows include the large boulder lags found at Grand Lake and Lake Travers. Glaciofluvial sediments, or "outwash," were also deposited beyond the ice margin, creating relatively level plains such as those found at Lake Travers, Lake of Two Rivers and Basin Lake. The Lake Travers area is considered a provincially significant assemblage of ice-contact, glaciofluvial, fluvial and eolian features unequalled anywhere in the Park. Notably, it has an inland dune field that was formed by strong prevailing winds acting on the outwash sands. The dune field includes transverse as well as longitudinal dunes now stabilized by vegetation. "Kettle" lakes, such as McKaskill Lake, were also formed when stranded blocks of ice melted after becoming buried or partially buried in sediment. Algonquin Park also has recent deposits such as beach ridges, offshore deposits, modern fluvial deltas, tombolos, talus cones and river flood plains.

The protection of these sites contributes to representation of earth science features and processes by preserving some of the history of glacial Lake Algonquin. Provincially and regionally significant earth science sites have been designated Nature Reserve Zones to provide them with the highest form of protection. Larger assemblages, some regionally significant features, and small features of local significance are protected in Special Management Areas, Classes I (14,925 hectares) and II (41,985 hectares), within other Park zones (for further information see Sections 6.6, 8.1, 9.2) (Spek, 1993).

6.1.3 Life Science

The life science Nature Reserve Zones protect representative examples of different vegetation-landform complexes, forest types, wetland complexes, natural disturbance sites, watersheds, and exceptional flora and fauna.

Some examples of Nature Reserve Zones that protect significant **vegetation-landform complexes** include the Petawawa Rapids, Barron River Canyon, Brent Crater and Lake Travers Nature Reserve Zones.

The Petawawa Rapids Nature Reserve Zone (1927 hectares) is a provincially significant upland forest, lowland, and shoreline complex with more than 400 identified species of flora. It has the highest diversity of native flora, including 10 species found nowhere else in Algonquin and another 18 considered rare in the Park. The nationally rare Waterweed (*Podostemum ceratophyllum*), One-sided Rush (*Juncus secundus*), and Clinton's Bulrush (*Scirpus clintonii)* are among the few existing records of these species in the province. There are also relict northern taxa on cliff sites and relict southern taxa in sheltered valleys along the river. Significant fauna in this zone include a breeding population of the provincially vulnerable Wood Turtle.

The Barron River Canyon Nature Reserve Zone (1076 hectares) is a provincially significant upland forest and outcrop complex. The Barron River canyon consists of a series of spectacular gorges with granite walls towering more than 100 metres above talus slopes. The concentration of calcareous material along crevices and seepage areas has encouraged the growth of locally rare calcicolous plant species, such as Maidenhair Spleenwort Fern (*Asplenium trichomanes*).

Indian Pipe

A number of post-glacial relicts, such as the Encrusted Saxifrage (*Saxifraga paniculata*), have also persisted in this area since the canyon acted as a major postglacial drainage system. The nationally rare Purple Cliff-brake (*Pellaea atropurpurea*) and Slender Naiad (*Najas gracillima*) occur here as does the provincially rare Rocky Mountain Woodsia (*Woodsia scopulina*) and a number of locally and regionally rare southern taxa. The cliffs of the canyon offer nesting habitat for a variety of birds, including the Barn Swallow, Common Raven, and Eastern Phoebe.

The Brent Crater Nature Reserve Zone (1199 hectares) is situated at the site of an ancient meteor crater. It contains a considerable amount of calcareous substrate, which supports locally rare bryophyte and herbaceous species, including one of the few Algonquin Park sites for Bulblet Bladder Fern (*Cystopteris bulbifera*). This site has a number of locally and regionally rare calcicolous plants and the only record in the Park of the Eastern Ground Pine (*Lycopodium obscurum*).

The Lake Travers Nature Reserve Zone protects a provincially significant earth science sand dune complex. Situated on the dune complex is a provincially significant upland forest of Red Pine and Jack Pine. The undergrowth is sparse and dominated by drought-resistant shrubs and grasses and includes such provincially rare species as Bulbostylis (*Bulbostylis capillaris*) and the nationally rare Sand Jointweed (*Polygonella articulata*).

The zone also includes the shallow warm-water bays of Lake Travers, which support a variety of aquatic vegetation, particularly dune-marginal aquatic systems not represented elsewhere in the site district.

Nature Reserve Zones also represent specific **forest types**, such as the Rana Lake Red Oak Nature Reserve Zone, a provincially significant forest containing the most extensive, mature stand of Red Oak *(Quercus rubra)* in Algonquin Park. Similarly, the Dickson Lake Hemlock Nature Reserve Zone has been designated to protect a provincially significant upland forest of mature Eastern Hemlock estimated to be more than 300 years of age mixed with large Red Pine of approximately 340 years of age (the oldest trees known in the Park). The Big Crow White Pine and Anglin-Dickson White Pine Nature Reserve Zones are provincially significant upland forests designated to protect tolerant hardwood forests of Sugar Maple, American Beech, and/or Yellow Birch in which 35- to 40-metre-high ancient White Pine of 80 to 120 centimetres in diameter are distributed. These zones are the best examples in Canada of the White Pine-tolerant hardwoods association that once dominated vast areas of the Great Lakes-St. Lawrence Forest Region prior to the arrival of the first loggers. Other zones, such as the Carl Wilson White Pine, Carcajou Jack Pine, and Bruton and Clyde Red Spruce Nature Reserve Zones, have been set aside to protect other representative forest types.

The Nature Reserve Zone system includes provincially significant **wetland** complexes, such as the Grand Lake Marsh, Cameron Creek Bog, Hogan Lake Mog (marsh-bog) and Hailstorm Creek Nature Reserve Zones, and provincially significant peatland complexes, such as the David Creek Bog and the Keegos Lake Bog. These areas provide breeding and migration locations for dabbling ducks, such as Mallard (*Anas platyrhynchos*), Blue-winged Teal (*Anas discors*), Green-winged Teal (*Anas carolinensis*), and Wood Duck (*Aix sponsa*). They also support uncommon reptiles, such as the Northern Water Snake (*Natrix sipedon*).

Many significant **wildlife species** have been observed in the Park's Nature Reserve Zones, including such uncommon wetland species as Virginia Rail (*Rallus limicola*) and Green Heron (*Butorides striatus*) and such uncommon

Hooded Merganser

boreal breeding bird species as the Lincoln's Sparrow (*Melospiza lincolnii*) and Yellow-bellied Flycatcher (*Empidonax flaviventris*).

The Nature Reserve Zones also contain some provincially and nationally significant plant species. These include the nationally rare Grassy Naiad (*Najas gracillima*) and Southern Twayblade (*Listera australis*), as well as the provincially significant White-Fringed Orchid (*Platanthera blephariglottis*), Hayden's Sedge (*Carex haydenii*), Triangle Grapefern (*Botrychium lanceolatum*), Flat Poverty Grass (*Danthonia lanceolatum*), and Rocky Mountain Woodsia (*Woodsia scopulina*). There are also a variety of locally significant species, including the Dwarf Mistletoe (*Arceuthobium pusillum*), Beach Heather (*Hudsonia tomentosa*), Lesser Bur-reed (*Sparganium natans*), Least Bladderwort (*Utricularia minor*), Beech-drops (*Epifagus virginiana*), Alpine Milkvetch (*Astragalus alpinus*), Yellow Bladderwort (*Utricularia gibba*), Smooth Cinquefoil (*Potentilla pensylvanica*) and Slender Cliffbrake (*Cryptogramma stelleri*).

Algonquin's Nature Reserve Zone System also protects sites of **natural disturbance**. The Tim River Burn Nature Reserve Zone protects an extensive open meadow and naturally regenerating forests on a site intensely burned by forest fires in 1922. The Merchant Lake Blowdown Nature Reserve Zone represents a site regenerating from an extreme wind storm in 1962.

Entire **watershed** units protected in the Nature Reserve Zone system include the Coldspring Watershed and the Greenleaf Creek Watershed Nature Reserve Zones. The large areas of these zones (4914 and 4041 hectares, respectively) protect the ecological integrity of the watersheds and preserve a cross-section of habitats, as well as floral and faunal elements. The Greenleaf Creek Watershed Nature Reserve Zone also protects ancient post-glacial fish and invertebrate fauna, some rare calcicolous floral species, the only southern Ontario record of the provincially rare Purple Reed-grass (*Calamagrostis purpurascens*), and the only certain site for the Algonquin Wood Fern (*Dryopteris x algonquinensis*), a hybrid between Fragrant Cliff-fern and Marginal Shield-fern.

6.2 Wilderness Zones

Wilderness Zones include wilderness landscapes of appropriate size and integrity that protect significant natural and cultural features and are suitable for wilderness experiences.

Wilderness Zones, which encompass 90,475 hectares of the Park, are protected and managed to preserve their natural state and provide recreational users with a semi-wilderness experience. Wilderness Zones were originally selected on the basis of their natural values and history of little disturbance. These zones contain natural and cultural resources, which are protected in the same way as Nature Reserve and Historical Zones. In addition, since Wilderness Zones protect entire landscapes, they permit the natural functioning of ecological processes. These areas also possess the least evidence of technological and industrial impact of man. Logging, railways, hydro lines, and buildings are all absent, and any disturbances are mainly attributed to such natural factors as wildfire, windthrow, insects, diseases, and wildlife.

Some existing activities in Wilderness Zones use motorized vehicles (e.g., ski-trail grooming, moose surveys, Algonquin Fisheries Assessment Unit studies and park maintenance). For each of these, the feasibility of eliminating the motorized vehicle or the activity itself will be examined.

The Algonquin wilderness

Facilities for these activities will include only those primitive types of recreational improvements, which are necessary for sanitation, fire and site protection, and for the protection and safety of users. Signs will be kept to the minimum required for safety and direction.

Algonquin Park currently has four Wilderness Zones: Burnt Island, Harness, Galeairy, and Lavieille-Dickson Lakes.

The largest Wilderness Zone, the **Burnt Island Wilderness Zone**, is a 48,870-hectare area located on the west side of the Park. Lying north of the Highway 60 corridor, almost on the summit of the Algonquin Dome (approximately 1700 metres), this rugged landscape contains many lakes, including several large ones. The zone is situated on a ground moraine landform, which includes an extensive area of kame (approximately 30%) and small areas of outwash and lacustrine landform. Mature tolerant deciduous and coniferous forests of Sugar Maple, Yellow Birch, and Eastern Hemlock exist on the thin-soiled rugged areas, whereas intolerant deciduous forests of Trembling Aspen and White Birch occur on ridge tops and in openings. Intolerant deciduous and mixed upland forests have developed on sites previously disturbed by fires (in the 1920s) in the western third of the zone.

On a granite lakeside cliff at the northern end of the zone, Peregrine Falcons had formerly nested, and with reviving populations of this species, this nesting site may become active once again. Existing development in the Burnt Island Wilderness Zone consists of historic ranger cabins, as well as portages and campsites along canoe routes.

The **Harness Lake Wilderness Zone**, a provincially significant landscape complex of 10,960 hectares lies south of the Parkway Corridor on the west side of the Park. Situated on the western flank of the summit of the Algonquin Dome, this area also receives more precipitation and has a slightly cooler microclimate than the east side of the Park. The zone consists of small lakes predominantly, disrupted creeks and non-forested wetlands scattered across a rugged ridge and valley terrain.

Located on a ground moraine landform, the zone's shallow soils of sandy-loam support primarily tolerant deciduous forests of Sugar Maple, American Beech, and Yellow Birch. There are also high proportions of tolerant coniferous Hemlock forest and intolerant coniferous forests of White Spruce (*Picea glauca*) and Balsam Fir. Deciduous swamps are rare in the zone and peatlands are relatively small and usually associated with boggy stream margins and lakeshores. Development in this zone is limited to portages and back-country campsites for Interior canoe routes and backpacking trails.

The **Galeairy Wilderness Zone**, the smallest Wilderness Zone at 5280 hectares, is located south of the Parkway Corridor on the east side. The zone consists of a ground moraine landform with thin, sandy soil and severely disrupted drainage at low elevations. As a result of early forest fires, dating from the 1920s, the major elements of the vegetation consist of intolerant coniferous and deciduous forests (White Pine, Red Pine, Trembling Aspen, White Birch) while the lower, mesic sites with deeper, loamy soils support tolerant deciduous forests of Sugar Maple, Yellow Birch, and American Beech. Occasional peatlands and deciduous swamp thickets occur along pond margins and in creek valleys. Development in this zone is limited to scattered back-country campsites along several small lakes and a cross-country ski trail.

The **Lavieille-Dickson Wilderness Zone** was established in 1993, following a recommendation from the 1989 Master Plan review, to study the provision of east-side representation of wilderness values in Algonquin Park. Within its 25,365 hectares, it contains the most outstanding remote backcountry on the east side of the Park.

This zone encompasses Lavieille and Dickson Lakes, as well as Little Dickson Lake, and provides back-country travellers with superb recreational values. This lake system is accessible from six different canoe routes and has spectacular scenery and an excellent trout fishery. Lavieille and Dickson are large, expansive lakes and provide a feeling of remoteness and solitude.

The Lavieille-Dickson Wilderness Zone contains the largest area (22,000 hectares) of landscape that has gone undisturbed for more than 50 years. This Wilderness Zone includes 21% (520 hectares) of the remaining old-growth Red and White Pine forests in the Park, and it ranks very high for the presence of other interesting and rare plants, and features of historical value.

All protective zones together (wilderness, nature reserve and natural environment) include 38% (955 hectares) of the old growth in the Park, thereby ensuring the representation of old-growth pine on the Park landscape. The remaining old-growth pine forest is located in scattered and small pockets in the Recreation/Utilization Zone. In this zone, a portion (7%) of the old growth is protected from harvesting through various forest management plan reserves. The remaining old growth, within the Recreation/Utilization Zone, is potentially eligible for harvest, provided it can be shown that overall old-growth diversity values are not adversely affected. This data will continue to be updated through the normal Forest Management Planning process.

6.3 Natural Environment Zones

Natural Environment Zones include aesthetic landscapes in which there is minimum development required to support low-intensity recreational activities.

The Natural Environment Zones in Algonquin Park total 13,765 hectares. Natural Environment Zones permit low-intensity recreational activities such as hiking, cross-country skiing, bicycling, horseback riding, fishing, backpacking, canoeing, and back-country camping. The five Natural Environment Zones in the Park are: Stratton Lake, Lake Travers, Oxtongue River, Fork Lake, and Sunday Lake.

On the east side of the Park, the **Stratton Lake Natural Environment Zone** (2215 hectares) consists of back-country campsites along the shores of Stratton Lake and the Barron River (**Figure 3**). This zone will continue to accommodate this type of recreational activity and interpretive trails.

The **Lake Travers Natural Environment Zones** (100 hectares), which are located between Lake Travers and Achray, are currently undeveloped (**Figure 3**). The future development of these zones will be restricted to interpretive trails.

The **Oxtongue River, Fork and Sunday Lakes Natural Environment Zones** (11,445 hectares) are all located along the Parkway Corridor. Currently, they all contain interpretive trails, cross-country ski trails and back-country campsites along canoe routes (**Figure 3**). Future development in this zone may include facilities for low-intensity recreational activities.

6.4 Historical Zones

Historical Zones include any significant historical resources that require management distinct from that in adjacent zones.

A camboose camp

Algonquin has a rich and varied human history, with traditional dependence upon the resources of the Park being a dominant theme. Extensive field research has identified more than 300 areas of historical human activity and a comparable number of archaeological sites. Those sites that provided the best representation of the Park's history were selected as Historical Zones.

The Historical Zone System, encompassing 1680 hectares, includes 48 historical sites and 38 archaeological sites. However, only the 48 Historical Zones (Appendix E) have been indicated on the zoning map (**Figure 3**); the rest, primarily archaeological sites, have not been identified to ensure their protection.

Sites range in size from a few hectares to nearly 400 hectares, as in the case of the Mowat Complex, a former town site. Historical features include depots and farms, relics of the timber trade such as camboose camps, segments of the former Ottawa, Arnprior and Parry Sound Railway and ranger cabins.

Archaeological sites represent primarily pre-contact period habitation or use such as shoreline campsites. These were used by successive Indian cultures in much the same way as they are by the Interior canoe-campers of today.

Future field work, study, and analysis will be conducted to complete a system of archaeological and historical sites. Until that time, all sites will be protected from disturbance.

The Park's Historical Zones are managed to protect them for future study and to provide an opportunity to enhance public understanding, awareness, and appreciation of Algonquin Park's heritage. Historical Zones protect these sites by excluding high-intensity uses, such as logging and campground development, and limiting low-intensity uses, such as trails, back-country campsites, or other interpretive developments. Some of the historical features (e.g., cabins) have been restored, and many artifacts and period pieces from some of the archaeological sites have been recovered, studied, and placed in the Park collections. Public information about site location is kept to a reasonable minimum, but in some cases the accessibility and quality of certain sites permit interpretation (see Section 8.6, Cultural Resource Management).

6.5 Development Zones

Development Zones provide the main access to the Park and facilities and services for a wide range of day use and camping activities.

There are five Development Zones in the Park, totalling approximately 22,545 hectares, which contain operational, research, recreational, and/or interpretive facilities.

Operational facilities include access point offices, campground offices, concessions, outfitters, and administrative offices. Recreational facilities in Development Zones provide overnight and day use opportunities suitable for a Natural Environment Park. These may include campgrounds, cabins and lodges, as well as day use facilities for picnicking, hiking, fishing, canoeing, boating, bicycling, cross-country skiing and horseback riding. Interpretive facilities can also be included in Development Zones to provide opportunities for visitors to learn more about the natural and historic values of the Park. These may include outdoor theatres, exhibit centres, museums or trails. For more information on the development of facilities (see Section 10.0 and **Figure 3**).

The Development Zones in the Park include the Parkway Corridor, Basin Lake, Achray, Brent, and Kiosk. The Parkway Corridor, located at the south end of the Park, is the largest and most developed zone. The four remaining Development Zones, located just inside the perimeter of the Park, are much smaller and provide access to the Interior recreational facilities (e.g., trails) and limited car camping opportunities. On the south-east side is the Basin Lake Development Zone, on the east side of the Park is the Achray Development Zone, and to the north are the Brent and Kiosk Development Zones. A Development Zone may also be considered near Kingscote Lake on the south side of the Park.

Future recreational developments and improvements will be designed to provide a greater variety of activities, improve the quality of services and facilities, and realign these facilities and services to ensure their support of Park goals and objectives.

There will be minimal provision of facilities to accommodate additional campers and trippers in the Parkway Corridor. Instead, development will be focused on the perimeter areas. The possibility of offering additional Natural Heritage Education programs at the development zones outside of the Parkway Corridor will also be examined.

The **Parkway Corridor Development Zone** follows the path of Highway 60 for 63 kilometres through the lower third of the Park. The total area of the Parkway Corridor is 21,145 hectares, excluding several Nature Reserve Zones that protect significant species or communities situated within the area. The Parkway Corridor Development Zone provides visitors with a "threshold" Algonquin experience. It contains an excellent cross-section of cultural, physiographic and biotic resources found throughout Algonquin Park, which can be appreciated through recreational as well as interpretive facilities and services. In the Parkway Corridor are campgrounds, picnic areas, trails (interpretive, bicycling, cross-country skiing, horseback riding), Visitor Centre, Education Centre, Theatre, Logging Museum, administrative buildings, information centres and offices for campgrounds and access points (see Section 10.0). The Park's Natural Heritage Education Program is almost entirely concentrated in this area of the Park (see Section 9.0).

The beach at the Achray campground

The **Basin Lake Development Zone**, composed of 756 hectares of land and water, includes Basin Lake and its surrounding shore. Recreational development consists of paddle-in and walk-in sites distributed along the lakeshore.

The **Achray Development Zone**, approximately 578 hectares, is situated on the north-east side of Grand Lake and includes two Interior lakes, Berm and Johnston Lakes. The abandoned CN railway right-of-way extends through this zone, paralleling the shores of Grand Lake. A campground is located along the shore of the lake bordering two fine natural beaches. There is also an administrative office, campground maintenance buildings and two historical

The cabins at Brent

sites (the Tom Thomson cabin and Tom Thomson Jack Pine site) in this zone. An interpretive trail extends around Berm Lake, and the adjoining Eastern Pines Backpacking Trail visits Johnston Lake and High Falls Lake, and provides several back-country camping opportunities.

A cabin at Kiosk

The **Brent Development Zone** consists of two areas of shoreland, 14 hectares and 9 hectares respectively, located south of the abandoned railway right-of-way and separated by the Brent townsite. An Historical and a Nature Reserve Zone are also located in the vicinity. Campground facilities that currently exist on each parcel of land will be upgraded and expanded.

The most northern development zone, the **Kiosk Development Zone**, is located on the north shore of Kioshkokwi Lake and encompasses the entrance to the Amable du Fond River. The abandoned CNR right-of-way cuts through this 43 hectares of land, separating three points of shoreline from the open fields of the former Kiosk townsite. An access point office, historic ranger cabin, boat dock and launch, and campground occupy one of the shoreline areas. Upgrading of the existing campground facilities and further campground and cabin development may occur in this zone.

6.6 Access Zones

Access Zones serve as staging areas where minimum facilities support use of Nature Reserve and Wilderness Zones and less-developed Recreation/Utilization, Natural Environment, and Historical Zones.

Access Zones, which make up approximately 735 hectares of the Park area, provide a valuable means of controlling and dispersing use in a manner most compatible with the purpose and values of the Park. Access Zones have been established along all public roads and around all access points in the Park that are not already contained within a Development Zone.

Access to Algonquin Park is gained by 29 access points located along Highway 60 (the Frank MacDougall Parkway) and around the perimeter of the Park Interior. These access and departure points consist of nine Interior access points located along Highway 60, 20 access points around the perimeter of the Park and eight departure points along rivers located both inside and outside the Park. However, only those access facilities located within the Park boundaries have been designated as Access Zones.

There are 10 Access Zones in the Park that incorporate one or more access points. The 10 zones are Rain Lake, Magnetawan, Kiosk, Brain, Brent, Achray/Lake Travers, Basin, Shall, Kingscote, and the Parkway Corridor (**Figure 3**). These Access Zones encompass access roads and may also contain parking and washroom facilities, access point offices, boat launches, outfitter/concessions and research facilities.

The most westerly Access Zones (Rain Lake and Magnetawan) leading to Rain Lake, Magnetawan Lake, and the Tim River incorporate parking and sanitary facilities. Two northern Access Zones (Kiosk and Brent) include only the access roads that lead to their respective Development Zones. The other northern access zone (Achray/Lake Travers) and the south-east access zone (Basin) have parking facilities in addition to the access road. The Kingscote Access Zone is similar to the Brain and Basin Access Zones but also includes a boat launch.

The Achray/Lake Travers Access Zone encompasses the access road leading to Achray and Lake Travers, as well as the roads and associated parking facilities for McManus Lake, Sec Lake, and the departure point on the Barron River. In addition, an access point office at the Park boundary is included within this zone.

The greatest number of facilities is provided in the Parkway Corridor Access Zone. This zone incorporates the access roads leading to Sunday Lake and Opeongo Lake through a Parkway Corridor Natural Environment Zone, as well as an access road leading to Rock Lake in the Parkway Corridor Development Zone (**Figure 3**). Access point facilities include parking, boat launch, access point office, outfitter and research facilities located on the shores of Opeongo Lake. The future development or upgrading of existing Park access points is described in Section 10.2.

6.7 Recreation/Utilization Zone

The Recreation/Utilization Zone includes aesthetic landscapes in which there is minimum development required to support low-intensity recreational activities and which also provide for commercial forest management. To the greatest extent possible, they will be planned, developed and managed in accordance with the policies set out for Natural Environment Zones.

The Recreation/Utilization Zone in Algonquin Park encompasses 594,860 hectares, which is split into a northern and southern section, divided by the Parkway Corridor. Recreational and forest management activities occur in this zone.

The Recreation/Utilization Zone provides back-country low-intensity **recreational** activities, such as backpacking, canoeing, camping, hiking, horseback riding, dogsledding, and mountain biking through the development and maintenance of recreational facilities. Resource utilization takes place in this zone in a discreet manner so that there is minimal impact on the natural and cultural values of the Algonquin landscape shared with recreational users.

Resource activities such as forest management, hunting and trapping are managed on a sustainable basis. They are also integrated with low-intensity recreational uses by separating these activities in both time and place. Hunting and trapping are permitted within designated areas in the Recreation/Utilization Zone and only during specified time periods (see Sections 8.4 and 9.1).

Forest Management occurs in 73% of the Recreation/Utilization Zone (or 57% of the whole Park area). Areas excluded from operations include reserves for shorelines, earth/life science and cultural values, water, "non-productive" forest land, non-forested areas and islands. Within the forest management areas, activities are also modified

Canoeists in the Interior

to protect any additional identified resource values. Special management practices are followed in designated "modified cut" areas (7.5% of the total harvest area in the 1990–95 Forest Management Plan) and in Class I Special Management Areas (2% of the Recreation/Utilization Zone). Overall, forest management is strictly controlled and confined each year to a number of small areas located throughout the Recreation/Utilization Zone. During the period 1990 to 1996, an average of 7,500 hectares were harvested annually, equal to 1% of the Park area.

7.0 Administration

Administration of the Park requires the organization of staff, assets and programs to carry out the Park's management, development and operation. The administration of resource and recreational programs is carried out from the complex of offices located at the East Gate in association with permanent work centres located at the Pembroke District Office and Samuel De Champlain Provincial Park, as well as a complement of seasonal administrative facilities (see Section 10.6).

Algonquin Park is administered by a Park Superintendent with the support of a management team responsible for Natural Heritage Education, compliance/enforcement, capital development, support services, resource management and the operations of Highway 60 and the Interior. A variety of technical, professional and clerical personnel, as well as seasonal staff, service contractors, and the Algonquin Forestry Authority (AFA), carry out program delivery. In addition, the Friends of Algonquin Park, a charitable co-operating association, assists in operating some programs. Volunteers and special programs (e.g., Environmental Youth Corp and Ontario Ranger Program) also provide program support.

The old East Gate

8.0 Stewardship Policies

Since the Park's establishment in 1893, management policies have aimed at supporting recreational, educational, resource and research use while still protecting the natural environment of the Park. The stewardship of Algonquin Park includes the management of land, water, vegetation, wildlife, fish and cultural features.

8.1 Land

Policies for the management of lands in Algonquin Park range from broad management directives for land use to specific restrictions on the use of soils, minerals and aggregates.

All management or development proposals outside the Park boundary that may affect Park lands or values will be reviewed and approved prior to implementation (see The Park Perimeter, Section 5.3).

Within the Park, land resources are generally protected and managed through **zoning** (see Zoning, Section 6.0). For example, many significant earth and life science features, landforms or landscapes are protected within Nature Reserve and Wilderness Zones and logging may only occur in the Recreation/Utilization Zone.

The **work permit** process regulates specific land use activities inside the Park.

- A work permit is required under the *Forest Fires Prevention Act*, the *Public Lands Act* or the *Lakes and Rivers Improvement Act* for work carried out in Algonquin Park. This includes the construction of buildings, timber harvesting, roads, bridges and water-related facilities but excludes minor maintenance and repairs to existing facilities.
- All projects or activities are reviewed through the work permit process to ensure that there are no adverse effects on the Park's natural or cultural values.
- Park development projects are exempt from this process but the Ministry of Environment is given prior notification under the *Environmental Assessment Act*.
- Cottages and commercial leaseholders must also comply with standards for construction and development (see Appendices A and B).

8.1.1 Soils

Algonquin Park soils are derived mostly from glacial deposits, which have been influenced by the underlying bedrock of granitic gneiss found throughout the Park. Therefore, the Park's soils are sandy with a shallow to moderately deep covering of stony, silty sand on the west side and a deep mantle of sand and silty sand materials on the east side, where greater post-glacial soil deposition occurred.

Recreation site planning considers soil data for proper selection, maintenance and rehabilitation of campsites. The best site selection not only minimizes soil erosion and damage to stream and wildlife habitat but also ensures increased durability and reduced maintenance in the long term. Soil compaction and erosion is also considered in determining the most appropriate location for walking and backpacking trails.

- In areas that are susceptible to disturbance, techniques such as boardwalks and stairs are used to minimize the impact from visitor traffic.
- For timber harvesting activities, logging roads will be located and constructed to minimize erosion in accordance with the Ministry's *Environmental Guidelines for Access Roads and Water Crossings*. Mitigative techniques, such as reducing slope, installing culverts and sediment traps, using only coarse material in construction, and encouraging regeneration of vegetative cover, are used to minimize soil deterioration and to maintain natural water flows.

8.1.2 Minerals

Prospecting, staking out claims and the working of mines are prohibited.

8.1.3 Aggregates

The Park contains a variety of aggregate deposits. Aggregates include gravel, sand, clay, earth, stone and rock other than metallic ore. Aggregate extraction in Algonquin Park conforms to the draft policy *Aggregate Resource Management in Provincial Parks*.

- A long-range Aggregate Resource Management Plan will ensure the protection of significant Park values from extraction. It will address existing pits, location of aggregate materials, ecological impacts of pits, and controls and guidelines for pit operations and rehabilitation.

- **Extraction** of aggregates is permitted in the Recreation/Utilization Zone for the construction and maintenance of logging roads.
- Aggregates from inside the Park may not be used outside the Park.
- Aggregates for the construction and maintenance of provincial highways and Park maintenance and development projects will be supplied from outside the Park.

- **Permits** will be issued for aggregate extraction in the Park undertaken by the Algonquin Forestry Authority (AFA), the Ministry of Natural Resources and their contractors.

- **Pits** must be authorized and site plans approved by the Park Superintendent, and must be situated where they will not conflict with existing or potential recreational use or Park values.
- Pits are not permitted within 120 metres of a body of water, wetland, public road, railway right-of-way, portage or backpacking trail; or within 60 metres of an MNR-maintained ski trail, unless approved in an Aggregate Resource Management Plan.
- Prior to the completion of an Aggregate Resource Management Plan, aggregate pits within 120 metres of a body of water or wetland may be approved contingent upon the review of earth and life science studies of the area as well as hydrological and other environmental impact studies of the site.
- Aggregate pits must be developed in a manner that minimizes the disturbance of the site, makes it most accessible for other future operations, does not sterilize the resource and can be rehabilitated at the termination of its use.
- Maximum pit size will not exceed 1 hectare.
- Gravel pits used for the purpose of commercial forest management must be located in the Recreation/Utilization Zone in areas where they will not conflict with existing or potential recreational uses or Park values.
- In the construction of roads, fill may be taken within the road right-of-way but not below the water table.
- Borrow pits are permitted in accordance with the guidelines specified in Appendix F.
- The AFA will be responsible for the rehabilitation of pits, landings and other recent manmade openings where future use cannot be adequately demonstrated.
- Pit operation and rehabilitation will be carried out according to the *Aggregate Resources Act*, *Health and Safety Act*, as well as to any conditions established by the Park Superintendent (e.g., setbacks from roads). Operating conditions will reflect changes in Park policy, zone boundary changes and any environmental concerns.

- **Special Management Areas** (SMA), Classes I and II, have been designated to protect significant earth science features. Class I SMAs (14,925 hectares) include sites that require special management strategies to maintain their earth science values (see Appendix G). Class II SMAs (41,985 hectares) include sites that will require no additional protection measures because the earth science values are resistant to forest management activities (see Spek, 1993).

Within both classes of SMAs, the provincially significant or sensitive features have been designated Nature Reserve Zones. Regionally significant and less sensitive sites have been identified as "core" areas that would be protected from aggregate removal, road building, site preparation and clear cutting (see Sections 8.1 and 9.2).

8.2 Water

Algonquin Park has 2,456 lakes in 19 principal watersheds. The pattern and abundance of these water bodies are important for recreation. Since Algonquin is situated on some of the highest land in the region, it serves as the headwaters for all of the watersheds except one, the Tim River, which flows from the west into the Park.

Algonquin's lakes and rivers are important for recreation

On the west side of the Park are many uniformly distributed small lakes that link streams while the central area is dominated by larger lakes. On the eastern side, the waterways are largely associated with long, linear scarp patterns forming rivers and streams, which connect with the lakes in the central area. Water quality is excellent but visitors are cautioned about drinking untreated surface water.

Provincial legislation such as the *Environmental Assessment Act*, the *Environmental Protection Act*, the *Lakes and River Improvement Act* and the work permit process are important management tools. Through their use, Park waters are protected from any practices that may alter established water levels, reduce the supply of water, alter fisheries habitat or cause deterioration in the quality of water in the Park.

- A **Water Management Plan** will take direction from this plan for the monitoring and control of water quality and quantity. Managing water resources requires preservation of the high-quality waters and maintenance of the quantity and timing of flows that affect not only watershed storage but also the recreational, biotic and cultural resources both in the Park and downstream.

Water quality is protected through management and educational activities. In the Interior it is protected through the education of users; in the developed areas by adequate sanitation facilities and programs.

- Public and private facilities are monitored and unsatisfactory conditions rectified.
- All new installations must be approved by the Ministry of Environment.
- Soil erosion may also affect water quality, so shoreline protection measures such as bank stabilization are used to prevent siltation.
- The design and construction of any lakeshore and stream bank projects must also be compatible with the natural character of an area and use natural materials.
- Forest management restrictions such as shoreline reserves and procedures for stream crossings have been established to protect the quality of the water resources in the Park.
- Both the Ministry of Environment and the Ministry of Natural Resources carry out testing and monitoring for the effects of acid rain on the Park's waters.

Water quantity in the Park is managed through the operation, maintenance and construction of 10 weirs and 13 gated control dams.

Weir dams have a stepped overflow design to allow a high discharge at high river or lake stages and to maintain a low flow during all but the most severe drought.

For control dams, a pattern of drawdown and storage is followed to make water available for downstream use, as a measure of flood control to prevent shoreline or property damage and to sustain summer recreational uses and fisheries habitat. The water level created by gated dams will normally not be greater than the highest former high water mark.

- The operation of the Muskoka River Waterway System (which includes Joe, Ragged, Burnt Island, Tea, Smoke, and Canoe Lakes in Algonquin) is guided by a formal agreement with Ontario Hydro. If water management activities conflict with other resource management objectives, such as fisheries production, discussions are undertaken with Ontario Hydro and other interested groups to try to modify the water level manipulations and eliminate or reduce the adverse effects.
- Algonquin also forms the headwaters of the Madawaska River, and contributes water to an important hydro-electric and recreational waterway system downstream. The management of the Madawaska River (which includes such lakes as Source, Cache, Opeongo, Rock and Booth in Algonquin) is being reviewed by Ontario Hydro and Ministry of Natural Resources staff. The outcome of this review, which could include information sharing and communications, will be considered in the development of the Park's Water Management Plan.
- Where there is no agreement with Ontario Hydro and no significant impacts on recreational, biotic or cultural resources, dams will be allowed to disintegrate naturally and lakes will be permitted to return to their natural levels.

8.3 Vegetation

Algonquin Park, which lies within the Algonquin-Pontiac section of the Great Lakes-St. Lawrence forest region, consists of a mosaic of coniferous and deciduous stands. There is no significant north-south differentiation. Instead, the Park's topography creates an east-west climatic difference, which has the greatest influence on species representation in the Park.

At the top of the Lookout Trail

The **flora** may be grouped into several broad types of vegetation, distributed according to underlying physical features and modified locally by climate. Today, the forests growing on the high and rugged land of the western side of Algonquin Park are primarily Sugar Maple mixed with Yellow Birch, Beech, and Hemlock. On the east side of the Park, which is sandier, drier and more gently rolling, the forest is a mixture of poplars, White Birch, White and Red Pine, with the pines dominating. Disturbance history is also a contributing factor to species occurrence, as early fires and past logging practices may have changed the relative proportions of species in the Park. With improved fire prevention, detection and control, as well as sustainable forest management practices, these types of mass disturbances have been reduced and the forests of Algonquin have typically attained ages ranging from 80 to 140 years.

Vegetation management is carried out in the Park to sustain natural vegetation, encourage species diversity, remove non-native species, maintain species composition, provide a variety of successional stages and (in the Recreation/Utilization Zone) generate forest products.

Managing for these purposes involves non-commercial and commercial vegetation management, fire management and the management of particular forest conditions (e.g., insects and disease).

General management policies are provided in this section of the plan, but a **Vegetation Management Plan** will be produced to describe specific objectives and strategies for every type of zone in the Park.

8.3.1 Non-commercial Vegetation Management

Vegetation management policies have been developed for the cutting, planting, burning, or spraying of vegetation in all zones of the Park. In general, these activities must complement the purpose and permitted resource and recreational uses of all zones.

- The **cutting** of vegetation for general maintenance or safety reasons is permitted in all zones.
- Vegetation may be cut for the development or maintenance of portages, trails and campsites in Development, Wilderness, Nature Reserve, Historical, Natural Environment and Recreation/Utilization Zones.
- Any other cutting of vegetation in a Development Zone must be carried out according to an approved plan.
- In the Recreation/Utilization Zone, Park staff may not cut trees for use in maintenance activities or improvement projects closer than 180 metres from campsites, portages and the shores of canoeable bodies of water.
- The cutting of live vegetation by Park users is prohibited.
- The use of portable stoves for cooking will be encouraged to decrease the amount of site degradation from vegetation removal and to reduce the incidence of wildfires caused by campfires.
- Chainsaws are prohibited in the Park, except for maintenance and management purposes by leaseholders, contractors, the AFA, the MNR, researchers, Ontario Hydro, and the Ministry of Transportation as authorized by the Park Superintendent.
- Hand **planting** or seeding and cover manipulation using native species may be carried out on campground and Interior sites that require rehabilitation after heavy use or damage from insects, disease or fire.
- The introduction of **non-native species** is prohibited in the Park, with the exception of landscaping grasses and shrubs in the Development Zone. The replacement of non-native species with native species is encouraged.
- **Herbicides** may be used by Ontario Hydro and the Ministry of Transportation to control vegetation along their respective rights-of-way only in the Recreation/Utilization and Development Zones. The use of herbicides will be discontinued once an economically viable alternative for treating their rights-of-way has been found (e.g., planting native shrubs).

The intentional use of **fire** for the purposes of non-commercial vegetation management is described in Section 8.3.3 (Fire Management).

8.3.2 Commercial Vegetation (Forest) Management

The Algonquin Forestry Authority (AFA) was established in 1975 as a Crown Agency responsible for harvesting timber in the Park and supplying it to manufacturing facilities outside the Park. The AFA is directed by a general manager who reports to a Board of Directors, which approves all work plans and provides advice on a variety of issues.

A 20-year Algonquin Park Forestry Agreement between the MNR and the AFA (which is reviewed every five years) defines the AFA's obligations for such activities as plan preparation, silvicultural operations, harvesting and road maintenance. The AFA prepares a Forest Management Plan (FMP) describing in detail how it will undertake these forest management activities. The FMP is subsidiary to and must comply with the policies of the Algonquin Park Management Plan. The Ministry audits the AFA's operations to ensure that they are carried out in accordance with the management direction in both the approved FMP and the Park Management Plan. A summary version of the FMP is available to the public from the AFA.

Vegetation management for commercial purposes is permitted only within the Recreation/Utilization Zone and is subject to specific controls and standards outlined in forest management planning documents. The FMP, which is publicly reviewed, and its Annual Work Schedules describe how the AFA will manage the forests (in the Recreation/Utilization Zone) in terms of access, harvest, renewal and maintenance. The FMP also stipulates how a variety of successional stages, a diversity of vegetation communities and the natural character of the area will be perpetuated while contributing forest products to local economies.

Sustainable resource management is the objective for Algonquin Park; therefore, harvest levels prescribed in the FMP will reflect good forest management practices and not a specific volume. Approximately 1% of the Park is actively cut each year, primarily through silvicultural systems that maintain a continuous forest cover. The Ministry has also prescribed certain procedures for forest management operations that are designed to maintain aesthetic qualities for recreational users and to protect the significant features in the Park. This may include the use of no-cut reserves and/or modified operations and controls on location, standard and degree of development of roads and associated structures.

Forest management practices in the Park are carried out according to specific silvicultural and operating guidelines designed to encourage productive stand growth and regeneration while minimizing the impact of forest management operations. For example, the number of skid trails is minimized and they are aligned to minimize damage to remaining trees. Forest management guidelines also encourage the retention of naturally unhealthy trees, which are beneficial to the forest ecosystem, such as cavity-nesting birds.

A porcupine in a birch tree

Silvicultural systems vary with the nature and condition of the forest to achieve vegetation management objectives. These silvicultural systems also evolve over time as new techniques are developed. Currently, the silvicultural systems used in Algonquin Park include the selection system, uniform shelterwood system, and patch clear-cutting. The selection and uniform shelterwood systems are the principal silvicultural systems. The selection system is used primarily on tolerant hardwoods such as Sugar Maple or American Beech and the uniform shelterwood system is usually used on upland tolerant conifers such as White Pine. In these systems individual trees are selected for harvesting, thus maintaining a continuous forest cover, which encourages optimum regeneration. The third silvicultural system, clear cutting, is applied in patches to create openings for the establishment of (shade) intolerant species, such as White Birch and Trembling Aspen, which require an abundance of space and sunlight to regenerate.

The application of these systems also involves the use of tree-marking guidelines. These guidelines are used to identify which trees should be harvested and which trees should be retained to maintain an ecologically diverse forest. Marking guidelines are also used to preserve trees that serve as food for bears, nesting areas for birds and late winter shelter for deer and moose (see Section 8.4, Wildlife).

Forest management operations are described in Section 9.2.

8.3.3 Fire Management

Much of Algonquin Park has burned at least once in the last century and a half. In recent years, fire prevention measures have been successful in reducing fire occurrence, while increased detection and aggressive fire suppression techniques have kept burn areas low. Now, in a normal year, about 25 hectares burn in approximately 50 forest fires. The majority of these fires are caused by people while the rest are started by lightning. Although fire is a potential threat to the Park's resources and visitors, it also influences vegetation renewal and has been a major factor in the development of the present forest mosaic. Therefore, fire management is an important component of vegetation management in Algonquin Park.

The current goals and objectives of the fire program are contained in the Interim Fire Management Strategy for the Algonquin Fire Region and in the East Fire Region Fire Operations Plan. The basic policies on fire prevention, detection, suppression and management are as follows:

The **fire prevention** program in the Park is composed of education, engineering and enforcement. Education is the largest component and the most important of the three.

- Visitors are educated on safe campfire building and maintenance, the potential for fire and the hazards of fire.
- Visitors are encouraged to use portable stoves in the Interior as a means of reducing the incidence of recreational fires. The use of portable stoves also reduces site degradation caused by the removal of vegetation for campfires.
- Site design and maintenance involves the protection of values by the removal or reduction of hazards. For example, the construction of fire pits prevents the outbreak of fire.
- Enforcement is an integral part of forest fire prevention. Enforcement is based on the *Forest Fires Prevention Act* and the *Provincial Parks Act*. These acts deal with such matters as the responsibilities of persons using fires and measures restricting fire use and travel when fire danger and risk are extreme.

Fire detection is achieved by co-ordinating organized air detection patrols with routine flying by Ministry aircraft and by receiving reports of fires from the public and commercial aircraft. Fire weather stations located in and around the Park, as well as daily forecasts and fire weather index ratings supplied by the Regional Fire Centre, are used for predicting fire occurrence and behaviour. This information is utilized for daily fire prevention, detection and suppression planning purposes.

Fire suppression procedures are similar to those used elsewhere in the province and are described in a detailed Regional Fire Operations Plan. All fire suppression activities in the Park are carried out according to provincial fire policy.

- Fire suppression activities will be carried out in a manner that minimizes negative impacts on the Park's environment.
- Disturbances associated with fires and fire suppression in recreational areas may be rehabilitated by supplementing natural plant succession through seeding or planting native species. Visitor activity is also re-routed and the site left to regenerate naturally.

Fire management in the Park involves the use of fire, both natural and induced, as a means of attaining resource management goals.

- All fires in Algonquin Park will receive a suppression response.
- In Wilderness and Nature Reserve Zones, that response may be reduced to monitoring so that fires of natural origin may be permitted to burn as natural disturbances, provided they do not threaten visitor safety, recreational values or values in adjacent Park zones or areas outside the Park.

Prescribed burning is defined as the deliberate and skillful application of fire to forest fuels under pre-determined site and weather conditions to attain a specific resource management objective.

- Prescribed burns may be used in Nature Reserve, Wilderness, Development, Natural Environment, and Recreational/Utilization Zones in accordance with the *Ontario Prescribed Burn Planning Manual*, as well as other pertinent Ministry and Park policies, procedures, and plans.
- In Nature Reserve and Wilderness Zones, prescribed burning can be used to perpetuate fire-associated values and conditions represented in the zone.
- In Development, Natural Environment and Recreation/Utilization Zones, fire can be used to obtain both forest and wildlife management objectives, such as site preparation for planting, hazard reduction, maintaining or establishing areas for picking berries or enhancing species diversity and wildlife habitat.

8.3.4 Insects and Diseases

Insects and diseases are monitored on a continuous basis.

- The control of insects and diseases of plants is only permitted in the Park where there is evidence that lack of control will result in unacceptable losses of recreational or forest resources in Development, Natural Environment, or Recreation/Utilization Zones or cause unacceptable damage to resources in adjacent zones or outside the Park.
- The objective of insect and disease management is to prevent conditions that result in a need for biocidal control. Therefore, control action may involve preventing, retarding, suppressing, or eradicating incipient, potential, or emergency outbreaks.
- Biological control will be used wherever feasible.
- If the use of biocides such as insecticides or fungicides is required, only biocides and methods approved by the Ministry of Natural Resources and the Ministry of the Environment and that are not harmful to other forms of life will be used.
- Site restoration following a disease or an insect outbreak may be carried out for forest management, fire prevention or aesthetic reasons.

8.3.5 Acid Rain

Acidic precipitation may also affect the forest if combined with other stresses or if the area has limited buffering capacity. Acid rain is being monitored on a continuous basis in the Park by the Ministry of Natural Resources, the Ministry of the Environment and Forestry Canada. To date, there has been no serious impact detected on terrestrial or aquatic ecosystems that can be clearly attributed to acid rain.

- The acid rain monitoring program will continue to be encouraged in the Park.

8.3.6 Forest Research

The goal of the Ontario Long-Term Ecological Research (LTER) Program is to conduct long-term ecological research that is necessary for sustainable ecosystem management and to apply this information to MNR policy development.

- The existing forest research area at Swan Lake, and other areas in the Park, will continue to be set aside for research purposes to support this goal.

8.4 Wildlife

Algonquin Park is one of the best known "wilderness" areas in North America and is considered southern Ontario's principal wildlife area. The Park's geographical position in south-central Ontario, as well as its variations in elevation, climate, soils, vegetation and aquatic conditions, produce a diversity of biotic communities. These biological communities contain a variety of faunal species, which include approximately 134 breeding species of birds, 45 species of mammals, 14 species of reptiles and 16 species of amphibians.

A **Wildlife Management Plan** will contain management guidelines for the Park's wildlife and wildlife habitat. The objective of wildlife management in the Park is to foster the continued existence of the full array of native wildlife and their natural habitats, and to ensure that no vulnerable, threatened or endangered (VTE) species are extirpated by other than natural processes. At present, wildlife management includes a combination of population surveys and habitat provision, controls for hunting and trapping, animal control and research. Protection measures include zoning and the application of Ministry standards and guidelines in forest management operations.

- The plan will include general wildlife management policies, policies directed toward the protection of VTE species and their habitats, and policies for the protection of entire biotic communities.
- The plan will address ways in which fire and forestry can help to sustain the balance of wildlife diversity in the Park by maintaining a mix of early-, mid-, and late-succession forests.
- Wildlife management will focus on maintaining wildlife populations through habitat management and population surveys. In particular, species such as Moose, White-tailed Deer and Wolf, and those species recognized as provincially VTE are of special importance.
- Wildlife management objectives will be co-ordinated with the Vegetation Management Plan Objectives.

8.4.1 Wildlife Populations and Habitat

In general, the forest and recreation management carried out in the Park provides habitat for a wide variety of species. Also, species and habitat are protected through zoning in the Park Management Plan and through the use of wildlife guidelines in the preparation of the Forest Management Plan.

There have been 258 **bird** species recorded in the Park, of which 134 have been known to breed. These include such northern birds as the Gray Jay (*Perisoreus canadensis*), Boreal Chickadee (*Parus hudsonicus*), and Spruce Grouse (*Dendragapus canadensis*) and such southern species as the Indigo Bunting (*Passerina cyanea*), Brown Thrasher (*Toxostoma rufum*), and Wood Thrush (*Hylocichla mustelina*).

Thirty species of **reptiles and amphibians** have been identified in Algonquin Park, including the nationally rare Spotted Turtle (*Clemmys guttata*), the provincially significant Wood Turtle (*Clemmys insculpta*) and the Two-lined salamander (*Eurycea bislineata*).

There are 45 species of **mammals** in the Park. Although there are such locally significant species as the Northern Long-eared Bat (*Myotis septentrionalis*) and the Rock Vole (*Microtus chrotorrhinus*), larger species such as

Spruce Grouse

River Otter, Wolf, American Black Bear, Moose and White-tailed Deer are more popular subjects for recreational viewing and research.

Algonquin Park has one of the most southerly wolf populations in North America, with wolves being one of the major scavengers and predators in Algonquin. Wolf research was initiated as early as 1958 in the Park, ceased in the mid-1960s and resumed in 1985.

Although little information has been collected in Algonquin Park, it is believed that a healthy bear population exists in the Park, judging by the extensive area of favourable habitats and by population studies undertaken in similar habitats elsewhere.

The existence of both moose and deer in the Park illustrates the influence of the meeting of the northern boreal and southern deciduous hardwood forests in the Park. White-tailed Deer, an ungulate indigenous to areas south of central Ontario, extended its range into Algonquin as logging, farming, and natural forces such as fire altered the landscape, thereby creating more browse. During the past 30 years, the deer population has declined. Although the reasons are not entirely known, it is believed that the combination of habitat loss, severe winters and wolf predation led to this decline. The decrease in the deer population was subsequently followed by an increase in the moose population in the 1970s and '80s. This increase in moose may be attributed to the decrease in deer and therefore a decrease in the occurrence of the parasitic "brainworm" (*Parelaphostrongylus tenuis*). Brainworm, while harmless when carried by deer, can be lethal when transferred to moose.

Provincially **vulnerable, threatened and endangered** (VTE) species will be given priority in management decisions and activities. There are several vulnerable or endangered species that have occurred or still occur in the

Park. Considerable management effort has been employed on some of these. An attempt was made to reintroduce the Peregrine Falcon, a study of the Wood Turtle was initiated in 1987 and surveys have been conducted on the Red-shouldered and Cooper's Hawks. Currently, the following Park species are designated as: *vulnerable* (Wood Turtle, Eastern Hognose Snake and Red-shouldered Hawk), *threatened* (Short-jaw Cisco and Deepwater Sculpin) and endangered (none) by provincial and national ranking agencies (e.g., COSSARIO and COSEWIC). Further studies of VTE species will be encouraged and the existing provincial standards and guidelines for their protection and rehabilitation will continue to be applied during forest and park management activities.

The provincially threatened Wood Turtle

8.4.2 Hunting and Trapping

In 1961, the *Algonquin Park Extension Act* added Clyde and Bruton Townships to the Park specifically on the condition that hunting and trapping be permitted to continue. Therefore, any changes to these uses require the *repeal or amendment* of this Act. Because of the similarity of historical use in the McRae Addition (in Eyre Township), it has been managed the same as Clyde and Bruton Townships, with regard to these uses, since it was added to the Park in 1993.

Hunting is permitted in the Recreation/Utilization Zone in Clyde, Bruton and Eyre (McRae Addition) Townships. Hunting is also permitted in the east half of the Park by the Algonquins of Ontario (see Section 9.1 for details).

Trapping is permitted on registered traplines in the Recreation/Utilization Zone of Clyde and Bruton Townships and in the McRae Addition (Eyre Township).

- Trapping includes all species of Park furbearers except Wolf, Lynx and Bobcat, and management quotas have been set for each registered trapline.
- Licensed registered traplines in Clyde and Bruton Townships will be phased out once the *Algonquin Park Extension Act* is amended or as opportunities permit.
- Licensed registered traplines in the McRae Addition will be phased out as opportunities permit.

Since 1958, the Algonquins of Ontario have held trapping licenses on 19 registered traplines in the eastern and central parts of the Park.

- Trapping by the Algonquins of Ontario will continue in this area.

8.4.3 Animal Control

Animal control is carried out for the safety of visitors and to protect facilities or other Park values. The control of wildlife primarily involves bear, beaver or an animal behaving abnormally, such as one afflicted with rabies.

- Policies for the management of nuisance wildlife in the Park will be contained in the Wildlife Management Plan.

In general, management efforts are designed to minimize the problem through educating the public, modifying the factors that are affecting the behaviour of the animal, or disposing of the animal. For example, beaver control involves the removal of dams, installation of beaver "baffler" devices or trapping if necessary.

- Bear control requires that garbage along the corridor and perimeter access points be deposited in bear-proof garbage facilities.
- If a bear shows behaviour that conflicts with Park users, it is relocated or may be disposed of if relocation is not feasible or if the bear has a previous history of such behaviour.
- Visitors are informed and educated on how to effectively avoid creating conflicts with bears (e.g., securing food supplies).

Moose with calf

8.4.4 Wildlife Research

The Wildlife Research Station at Lake Sasajewun has made major contributions to wildlife research since 1944, including studies on mammals, birds, and invertebrates. As an important wildlife area as well as gene pool, the Park can also assist research projects that are attempting to re-establish viable populations of a locally extirpated species. In the past, the Park has provided moose and river otter in wildlife transfers to the states of Michigan and Missouri, respectively.

Vegetation studies in the Park also contribute to the development of new wildlife management strategies. For example, a study on the status and conditions necessary for hemlock regeneration and recruitment has important implications for wildlife because this tree species provides winter cover for moose and deer and is the single most valuable tree species for forest birds.

- Research on all species of wildlife in the Park will be encouraged so it may contribute further management information on Algonquin's wildlife populations (see also Section 9.6, Research).

8.5 Fisheries

Algonquin Park is one of the great natural fisheries in Ontario and the only major complex of intact native trout fisheries remaining in southern Ontario. Fishing has long been one of the primary recreational attractions of the Park, providing approximately 128,000 opportunities of fishing annually (an opportunity is defined as four hours of fishing). In the Interior, it is second only to canoeing as a principal recreational activity, and it is the number one activity in the spring.

The provincial significance of Algonquin's fisheries and its recreational value require that protection and sound management are equally important elements of fisheries management.

Lake Trout

The Park's harsh climate and the low productivity of its lakes limit the species composition and productivity of fish communities. Following the retreat of the glaciers 10,000 years ago, the five major watersheds of Algonquin were inhabited by such coldwater species as Lake Trout (*Salvelinus namaycush*) and Whitefish (*Coregonus clupeaformis*). The native trout communities that developed are still largely intact while the distribution of warm-water sport fish has expanded but remains limited.

Today, the Park has a total of 50 species of fish with the majority of the lakes containing cold-water species, of which Lake Trout and Brook Trout are the two principal species. Lake Trout occur in approximately 149 lakes, which are generally greater than 40 hectares. Brook Trout occur in 240 lakes but generally exist in smaller-sized lakes as well as streams and rivers. Warm-water species, such as Walleye (*Stizostedion vitrium*) and Muskellunge (*Esox maskinonge*), are primarily confined to the lower portions of the Petawawa watershed but are absent from the various headwaters in the Park. Historically, Smallmouth Bass (*Micropterus dolomieui*) were introduced into 85 lakes in the Park, primarily along or near the Parkway Corridor, and they have displaced the native Brook Trout from these waters. Northern Pike (*Esox lucius*) have gained entry into the Opeongo River watershed from Shall Lake to Booth Lake, and it appears that these fish have become established in this area.

Fisheries management, as described in the 1986 Algonquin Park Fisheries Management Plan, is concerned with managing the Park's fisheries to maintain species diversity and the high quality of fishing in the Park Interior, enhance fishing in the Parkway Corridor, and generally keep the harvest of fish within sustainable levels. In general, angling is permitted in all zones of the Park except in identified sanctuaries. However, the fisheries resources and angling pressures vary between the Interior of the Park and the Parkway Corridor. Therefore, two management strategies have been established for the Park's fisheries (also see Section 9.1.2, Fish- and Wildlife-Oriented Recreation).

8.5.1 Parkway Corridor Fisheries Management

In the high demand areas of the Parkway Corridor Development and Natural Environment Zones, fisheries management consists of regulations controlling seasons and possession limits and a limited stocking program. Experimental size limits, to protect breeding stock, have also been introduced to examine the potential of maintaining naturally reproducing populations of Lake Trout without losing angling opportunities.

Similarly, size limits for Brook Trout were introduced to lakes along the corridor and in the Interior to develop a very high-quality fishery and to promote the conservation of native trout stocks.

- In lakes with natural-reproducing Lake Trout and Brook Trout, replenishment will be by natural reproduction, thus eliminating a need to supplement populations with planted stock.
- For lakes without natural-reproducing populations, a stocking program relying heavily on Splake (a hybrid between Brook Trout and Lake Trout, which rarely reproduces itself in the wild) will continue on small lakes in the Corridor.
- Stocking programs will continue in lakes within the Parkway Corridor Development Zone where native fish populations will not be affected, or within one portage of this zone.

8.5.2 Interior Fisheries Management

In the Interior (the Recreation/Utilization, Wilderness, Historical, Nature Reserve, and Natural Environment Zones), the strategy is to maintain a very high-quality, low-intensity fishing experience. This is achieved through the control of angling activity (Section 9.1.2) and certain policies regarding stocking, fish introduction and habitat protection.

- Population replenishment will be by natural reproduction, thus reducing the need to supplement populations with planted stock (fish stocking).
- Hatchery-reared fish will be stocked only in Development Zones or within one portage of these zones.
- Any trout stocking in the Interior will be essentially for introduction, research or rehabilitation only and will use native stocks (fish of direct wild Algonquin stock origin, with the exception of Billy and Ryan Lakes).
- Billy and Ryan Lakes are heavily fished lakes and do not have natural trout populations. Those lakes are stocked with Splake supplied specifically for harvesting.
- The introduction of new species of fish will be prohibited.
- Warm-water (e.g., walleye) and non-native species will be impeded from further range extension where possible.
- Rare or unique fish such as the nationally significant Shortjaw Cisco (*Coregonus zenithicus*) and the provincially significant Spoonhead Sculpin (*Cottus ricei*) will be protected.
- Habitats sensitive to disturbance can be identified and protected by monitoring the effects of forest management activities (stream crossings) and control dams on fish habitat and through the identification of spawning sites.

8.5.3 Fisheries Research

The Park's fisheries management program is highly dependent on the research conducted at the Harkness Laboratory of Fisheries Research and the Algonquin Fisheries Assessment Unit.

Research programs have been concerned with both native and introduced sports fish species. In particular, the Lake Trout and the Brook Trout research programs have provided an important understanding of these species in Park waters, valuable management strategies, and improved fishing opportunities. Studies are currently being conducted to fully document the distribution of all fish species in the Park and to identify unique genetic strains of Brook Trout that may be important to future management.

- Research of Algonquin's fish resources will continue to include the surveying of lakes and streams and the collection of other basic data on fish populations and habitat for the purpose of enhancing the fisheries management program in Algonquin.
- The effects of acidic precipitation or invasions of foreign aquatic species, such as the Zebra Mussel, on the Park's fisheries will also continue to be monitored.
- Future research may identify that further measures for the protection of Algonquin's fisheries are required. As a result, additional angler limitations, such as means of access, seasons, size limits or angling methods, may need to be implemented to preserve the quality of the fishery.

8.6 Cultural Resources Management

Considerable research effort and documentation have been undertaken to gain a better understanding of humans and the Algonquin environment. Field research in past years has identified more than 300 areas of historical significance and a comparable number of archaeological sites. The management direction for these sites is to preserve the most representative sites of historical or archaeological significance in an Historical Zone System and to protect the rest as areas of concern. Both designations protect the core features for future study and interpretation, but the Historical Zone provides more buffering and its policies on permitted activities are more restrictive.

The present **Historical Zone** System, which consists of 48 historical sites and 38 archaeological sites, prohibits timber harvesting activities and restricts certain recreational uses within each zone. All other sites are areas of concern.

- Historical and archaeological sites in the Recreation/ Utilization Zone will be designated as areas of concern with various strategies for protection, according to the *Forest Management Guidelines for the Protection of Cultural Heritage Resources*. Depending on the historical value, timber operations may be conducted with mitigation measures, modified or excluded from the sites.

- Historical and archaeological sites identified within the Development Zone and that have not been accorded an Historical Zone designation will be designated as areas of concern and protected from high-impact developments or activities such as campgrounds.

A **Cultural Resources Management Plan** will be completed which will provide an assessment of historical and archaeological sites and outline management guidelines for these sites. The development of this plan will be guided by the *Algonquin Region Historical Systems Study*, completed in 1980. Archaeological sites will be evaluated to determine which should be designated for preservation and what management practices are required. A revised system of historical sites will also be established based on the interpretive potential, representativeness, structural remains and historical significance of candidate sites. A major focus for historical resources interpretation is the new Algonquin Logging Museum near the East Gate, where structures and implements of the period are on display (see Section 10.4).

- The Park protects all newly discovered historical resources dating prior to 1940, pending thorough study and documentation of their significance.
- Complete photographic documentation of structures that are to be removed or destroyed is undertaken where feasible.
- For the management of archaeological resources, field research and the reconstruction of archaeological sites are only permitted by recognized authorities in the field of study.

Tom Thomson's cabin at Achray

- The location of archaeological sites need not be revealed until an examination and evaluation of the site is completed. In special cases, the locations of fragile sites may be withheld.
- All collected or donated information, artifacts and other materials related to historical and archaeological resources will be stored in the new Visitor Centre archival collections.
- The *Provincial Parks Act* prohibits the removal by the public of any artifact from the Park or the disturbance of any site of archaeological or historical interest.

9.0 Operations Policies

"Operations" refers to the provision of services required to operate the Park on a day-to-day basis. These services will be carried out according to a Park Operating Plan. This Plan will be prepared to provide Park staff with the necessary information required to operate the Park. In addition to addressing the operations policies which follow, the Plan will include such topics as budget, staffing, maintenance schedules, enforcement and emergency services. The Plan will be consistent with: the Ontario Provincial Park Operating Standards, Ontario Provincial Parks Policy and Procedures, the *Provincial Parks Act* and Regulations, and will be reviewed annually and updated as required.

In addition, specific restrictions on forest management operations are described in Section 9.2 that are designed to protect natural, cultural, and recreational values in the Recreation/Utilization Zone.

The *Provincial Parks Act* and Regulations permit the use of structures, installations, improvements, aircraft, motor boats, and logging, road building and other motorized equipment for Park management or operational purposes. However, all activities are scheduled and conducted in a manner that least conflicts with other recreational users and conforms as closely as possible to restrictions placed on the public. Overall, a comprehensive system of operational personnel and facilities is required to operate a park the size and complexity of Algonquin. These operations will be detailed in the Park Operating Plan for both the developed areas and the Interior, described as follows.

In the **Development Zones**, operations consist of facility administration, Natural Heritage Education, facility maintenance and recreation management. These operations are carried out by either Park staff, contracted services, co-operating associations or volunteers (e.g., host and hostess program).

- Facility administration includes reservations, registration, entry control and information delivery.
- Natural Heritage Education describes all visitor-oriented services and may include information delivery, marketing and programmed visitor activities.
- Facility maintenance may consist of waste management, sanitation, building cleaning, and ground, road, parking lot and general building/facility maintenance, utility operation (e.g., water distribution) and the auditing of concessions/contracts (e.g., firewood, laundry, stores and outfitters).
- Recreation management deals with the provision of management information (e.g., motor horsepower restrictions), security and enforcement.

Canoe Lake station

The **Interior** of the Park has five types of park operations: access points, Natural Heritage Education, Interior management, recreation management and stewardship. These operations may be carried out by the Ministry, the private sector through contracts/agreements or volunteers (e.g., youth camps).

- The maintenance and operation of Interior access points include: selling permits, providing information, maintaining offices and parking areas, as well as operating the office, fee stations and campgrounds (where applicable).
- Natural Heritage Education involves: providing information and counseling for Interior travelers.
- Interior management includes: maintaining and developing portages, backpacking trails and campsites.
- Recreation management involves: providing information and counseling travelers, enforcing Park regulations and rendering assistance in emergency situations.
- Stewardship operations are carried out in fisheries, wildlife and forestry management programs and may include activities such as creel and wildlife surveys or forest harvesting operations.

Many of these Park operations will be described in more detail in a Park Operating Plan or in other documents such as a Natural Heritage Education Strategy or a Marketing Strategy. The following sub-sections outline the basic direction for many of these operations, including: recreation management, forest management, compliance monitoring and enforcement, Natural Heritage Education, marketing/tourism and research.

Operations Policies

9.1 Recreation Management

Recreation for visitors to Algonquin can mean car camping along the Parkway Corridor, enjoying day use activities or experiencing the Interior or "wilderness" of Algonquin. Since the Park's establishment in 1893, recreational and resource management policies have been aimed at protecting and perpetuating its natural qualities.

In Development Zones, the aim of recreation management is to provide overnight and day use recreational opportunities without creating visitor congestion or detracting from the area's natural qualities.

Interior management is aimed at providing back-country recreational opportunities while preserving and perpetuating the characteristics of the Algonquin Interior "wilderness" experience. Wilderness is described as a characteristic of the land, a distinctive atmosphere that can be readily recognized or felt by a person visiting that land. A "wilderness" experience includes solitude, natural qualities and the absence of human, technological or industrial impact, such as roads, garbage and motors. In the Interior of Algonquin, Wilderness Zones and Nature Reserve Zones offer these types of experiences. The Recreation/Utilization Zone also attempts to preserve these characteristics through special forest management strategies.

Portaging in the Algonquin wilderness

Interior management strategies are designed to mitigate conflicts between users (such as canoeists and motorboat users) and place controls and regulations on other uses (e.g., forest management). In this way, the integrity of the Park environment is maintained to the maximum degree possible while still providing for visitor uses and needs. For example, to reduce conflicts between users in some lakes, motorboats are prohibited during the peak summer period to preserve the "wilderness" feeling for canoeists, but then are permitted during spring and fall when fishing is the more popular activity. More detailed information on basic recreation management policies for such activities as camping and hiking, fish and wildlife-oriented activities, and motorized and mechanical activities is described as follows.

9.1.1 Camping and Trail Recreation

Camping areas and trail systems provide opportunities to enjoy the natural features or scenic areas of the Park. The design and monitoring of camping areas and trail systems are important to protect the quality of a visitor's experience and the environment. Park values and visitor safety are also maintained through education, information, procedures, controls and regulations.

Campsites located in campgrounds, along backpacking trails or canoe routes are planned, developed, maintained, rehabilitated, reserved, closed or otherwise regulated to ensure protection of the resources.

- Guidelines for developing, maintaining and rehabilitating campsites will be included in an Operating Plan. The guidelines will prescribe the number of campsites to be distributed in a campground area or on an individual route or backpacking trail based on the social, ecological and physical carrying capacity of the area.
- Campsites are rehabilitated where necessary to ensure a quality experience and to prevent resource damage.
- Existing campsites may be closed where continued use will cause significant degradation of vegetation, soil or water quality or substantial conflict with other users.

Trail systems may be developed and/or designated for backpacking, day hiking, bicycling, horseback riding, dogsledding and cross-country skiing in appropriate zones.

- Trails are constructed and maintained to minimize conflicts between users, allow reasonably safe travel, and minimize soil erosion and damage to streams and wildlife habitats.

Recreation capacity is established to ensure the protection of the environment and the visitor experience, to reduce conflicts between users, and for safety purposes.

Development Zones provide camping and day use facilities for a large concentration of visitors.

The Interior's carrying capacity is much lower; therefore, the introduction of large numbers of users would erode basic wilderness qualities even with careful management of the resources and visitors.

Interior recreation management policies are directed toward developing and implementing a program to regulate and distribute Interior users, guard against overuse and minimize conflicts between users.

- Matching the number of Interior canoe trippers and backpackers with the supply of campsites is achieved through the Park reservation system. The operation of the system is described on the Park's canoe route map and in the Interior tabloid.

Management of recreationists is carried out through education and enforcement of the *Provincial Parks Act*, its Regulations, and other associated legislation (see also Section 9.3, Compliance Monitoring and Enforcement). Information contained in printed material, such as tabloids, signs or maps, is the principal means by which users are educated on the management controls for specific recreational activities. Personal contacts are also an important and essential means of delivering this information.

- In campgrounds:
  - ⇨ Campers are educated on particular management concerns such as the cutting of live growth, removing natural objects, littering or creating a disturbance to other users.
- In the Interior:
  - ⇨ Camping is permitted only on designated sites.
  - ⇨ Campers are required to carry out all non-burnable refuse in litter bags distributed to them.
  - ⇨ Interior travellers are prohibited by regulation from possessing non-burnable food and beverage containers other than containers specifically designed and intended for repeated use and for which no deposit is charged.
  - ⇨ To minimize conflicts between motor boats and canoeists, motorboats are restricted to certain lakes and have horsepower restrictions (see Section 9.1.3).
  - ⇨ Water skiing and all other related activities are prohibited in the Park.
  - ⇨ From April 1 to Thanksgiving, the possession of a gasoline generator, radio, cassette player or other electronic audio device, except a personal listening device, is prohibited in any area other than an organized campground or leasehold, except for maintenance and management purposes by leaseholders, AFA, Ministry, researchers, Ontario Hydro and the Ministry of Transportation as authorized by the Park Superintendent.
  - ⇨ Chainsaws are prohibited in the Park except for maintenance and management purposes by leaseholders, contractors, AFA, MNR, Ontario Hydro, researchers and the Ministry of Transportation as authorized by the Park Superintendent.
  - ⇨ New measures to reduce garbage in the Interior may be introduced.
  - ⇨ Visitors will also be encouraged to utilize portable stoves in the Interior as a means of reducing the incidence of recreation-caused fires and lessening the demands on the natural dead wood supply adjacent to heavily used campsites.

Rock climbing areas will not be designated in Algonquin Park. The *Provincial Parks Act* provides that no person shall rappel or climb rock faces in a provincial park with the aid of ropes, anchors or similar equipment except in an area designated for that purpose.

Canoe on a rocky point

Safety is important in recreation management and is considered in the development of all facilities and in the operation of the Park.

- The Park has some standard emergency procedures for first aid responses and forest fires, which are available 24 hours a day.
- First aid equipment and telephone or radio assistance are available in all offices and carried by Interior crews.
- Aircraft may be used in emergency situations.
- Search and rescue operations are the responsibility of the Ontario Provincial Police, and Ministry staff assist when requested.
- The proximity of wildlife to Highway 60 creates a safety concern for motorists travelling the highway. Road accidents most frequently involve moose and deer at night. This type of collision will be mitigated through the placement of warning signs and a reduction in road salt pools.

Forest management practices are modified to minimize adverse effects on visitors, the recreational resources and the natural values of the Park.

9.1.2 Fish and Wildlife-Oriented Recreation

The strategies for managing fish and wildlife populations in the Park were discussed in Section 8.0 (Stewardship). However, equally important, recreational activities that influence or are influenced by fisheries or wildlife populations must also be managed in order to maintain the health of these populations.

Wildlife viewing opportunities exist along the Parkway Corridor where wildlife is quite accustomed to the presence of people and in the Interior where they may be viewed in their natural habitat. Visitors may see such animals as moose, deer, beaver, otter and a variety of birds.

The wolf, an elusive animal in the Park, is appreciated through "wolf howls," a late summer interpretive event that enables visitors to hear howls from a nearby wolf pack.

- Viewing areas may be developed on the east side of the Park and along the Highway 60 corridor to facilitate this recreational and interpretive activity, as well as to ensure the safety of visitors pursuing this activity.

Public **hunting** activities have been permitted in the Recreation/Utilization Zone of Clyde and Bruton Townships since 1961 and the McRae Addition since 1993. In response to local public concerns, this use will not change at this time and will be permitted to continue at this time.

- Clyde, Bruton and Eyre Townships are managed to provide public hunting opportunities for most game species (e.g., small game and deer, moose and bear).

Timber Wolf

- The hunting of wolves will not be permitted in the Park.
- During specified seasons, hunting is permitted in designated day hunting areas and out of hunt camps under appropriate permits. Designated day hunting areas include the 3.2-kilometre wide strip centred along the hydro line right-of-way in Clyde Township, a 3.2-kilometre wide zone bordering Kingscote Lake and the McRae Addition.
- Possession and use of firearms is allowed in the Townships of Clyde, Bruton and Eyre (McRae Addition) or by trappers during open seasons, as provided by the *Game and Fish Act* and Park policy.
- The possession of firearms by the public in the rest of Algonquin Park is prohibited except when transported in a vehicle on Highway 60, where they must remain unloaded and encased.
- The balance of the Park will remain closed to hunting and the possession of firearms, except where authorized under the provisions of special agreements with the Algonquins of Ontario.

Hunting is carried out by the Algonquins of Ontario in the east half of the Park under the provisions of the **'Algonquin Hunting Agreement'**. The Agreement covers such matters as hunting areas, species, harvest numbers, sex/age ratios, monitoring, enforcement and reporting of the harvest. Agreements have been negotiated each year since 1991 pending the outcome of negotiations of the Algonquin's land claim.

Fishing is permitted in Algonquin Park only within regulated seasons from the last Saturday in April to the end of November. However, in several identified fish sanctuary waterbodies, fishing is prohibited year-round.

In the Parkway Corridor, heavily fished areas require more intensive management to provide fishing opportunities on a sustained basis. Fisheries management initiatives to control angling pressure include:

- Experimental regulations that restrict the size of fish caught have been established on selected Lake Trout lakes and two Brook Trout lakes. The effect of these regulations is being closely monitored.
- The publication and enforcement of all fisheries regulations (especially on lakes with special regulations) will encourage compliance.
- Smallmouth Bass fishing is also being promoted to relieve pressure in Lake Trout lakes.

In the Interior, where the Park contains more than 300 lakes with native trout populations, the focus of management is to protect self-sustaining native trout populations while providing high-quality, low-intensity fishing.

- Management of recreational fishing activity requires that access to the Interior remain limited and that fishing limits (including experimental size limits) be enforced.
- Angling pressure is controlled through conventional catch limits and experimental regulations restricting the size of fish caught on selected Brook Trout lakes. Those lakes subject to experimental regulation are under intense study to monitor any changes in the fisheries.
- Changes in the Interior access quota will require an assessment of the impact of the change on the fishery of the area.
- Enforcement and education, as key management devices, will encourage compliance to all fishing regulations.
- The Algonquin fishery is protected from introductions of undesirable competing species through a ban on the use and possession of live bait fish (including crayfish) in Park waters, as well as a ban on organic bait (only lures are permitted) in certain lakes subject to experimental regulations (also see Section 8.5, Fisheries).

9.1.3 Transportation of Recreationists

Transportation is restricted to motorized or mechanical transport on designated roads, waters, and land routes. In areas away from public roads, visitors must rely primarily on muscle power as a means of transportation. In doing this, the carrying capacity of the Park is increased and there is a better chance of visitors relating to Algonquin's environment and values. In addition, protection is afforded biotic and physical resources.

- Away from public roads, transportation is restricted to trails, portages, and waterways by means of foot, canoe, hand carts, and, where designated, bicycles, horses and dogsleds.
- Cross-country skiing and snowshoeing are not limited to designated travel routes.
- Permission to travel on other than designated roads, waters and land routes by motorized or mechanical transport is by permit only, issued by the Park Superintendent.
- These regulations do not apply to Ministry staff in the management of the Park or during emergencies.

To maintain the natural qualities of the Park and to protect its resources, mechanized and motorized travel are restricted to certain areas of the Park.

Mechanized travel refers to the use of devices that rely on non-motorized means of propulsion.

Taking a lunch break

- The use of horses and horsedrawn carts to haul boats, fishermen, camping equipment and fishing gear is currently restricted to the road joining the Lake Travers road and White Partridge Lake. Use of this travel route and campsites on White Partridge Lake is managed through the reservation system.
- Bicycles, hand carts and dogsleds are permitted only on designated routes.

Motorized vehicles are prohibited in Wilderness, Nature Reserve and Historical Zones except in emergencies or for park management purposes.

- In the Access, Development, Natural Environment and Recreation/Utilization Zones, public use of motorized or mechanical transports designed for use on snow, ice, land or water is permitted only on designated trails, roads and water routes. Authorization to travel on other than public routes is only by permission of the Park Superintendent.
- Motorized means of transport for emergencies or for administrative, research, forest management and harvesting activities and for hydro line and right-of-way maintenance is permitted in the appropriate zones with prior authorization by the Park Superintendent. Motorized travel is minimized within practical limits and care is exercised to avoid conflicts with recreational users.
- Hunters in Clyde, Bruton and Eyre (McRae Addition) Townships may use motor vehicles to travel Interior Park roads as described in the annual *Rules and Regulations for Hunting: Algonquin Provincial Park.*

- **Snowmobile** use by the public is permitted only along the hydro line corridor in Clyde and Eyre Townships, to provide winter access between Whitney and the Haliburton area, and along the section of the Haliburton snowmobile trail network that runs along the eastern side of the south boundary of Bruton Township.
- Leaseholders and landowners or their designate may, upon request, be permitted by letter of authority to travel by snowmobile to conduct essential maintenance functions.
- Snowmobiles may be used by trappers and contractors as authorized by the Park Superintendent.

- **Motor boat** use is limited to 38 lakes by regulation. Motor boats with unlimited horsepower are permitted only on Opeongo and Galeairy Lakes. The remaining

A snowshoer pulling a toboggan

36 lakes and portions of the Crow River have limits of 20 hp or less (see **Table 1**).

- Youth camps, lodges, outfitters, concessionaires and others doing business are exempted from the horse-power limit for utilitarian purposes (the movement of supplies or passengers) as approved annually by the Park Superintendent.
- No person will be permitted to leave a boat unattended or permit a boat owned by him or her to be left unattended in Algonquin Park except on the lakes and at the locations designated by the Park Superintendent, as described in **Table 2**.
- All boats must be removed at the completion of each trip.
- Boats may be left unattended overnight in organized campgrounds and on leased and patented lands.

Table 1. Motor Boats
Motor boats are permitted only on the following Algonquin lakes.

a) Motors of unlimited horsepower	
Galeairy	Opeongo
b) Motors of 20 horsepower or less	
Bonita Cache Canoe Cedar Kingscote Kioshkokwi Little Cauchon	Rock Smoke Source Tanamakoon Tea Two Rivers Whitefish
c) Motors of 10 horsepower or less	
Cauchon Cauliflower Grand Joe Little Joe Madawaska	Manitou North Tea Radiant Rain Tepee Travers
d) Motors of 6 horsepower or less *(except from the last Friday in June to the first Monday in September inclusive)*	
Big Crow Crow River from Proulx to Little Crow Hogan La Muir	Little Crow Proulx White Partridge

- The use of watercraft as floating living quarters is prohibited.
- Water skiing and other related activities (e.g., jet skiing) are not permitted on any waters in the Park.
- **Private aircraft** use in the Park is not permitted.
- **Military** land exercises are prohibited in the Park. The Ministry and the Canadian Forces Bases in Petawawa and Trenton also co-operate to minimize the impact of low-level flights on Park recreational users.

Table 2. Caching of Motor Boats and Canoes
*Canoes and boats may **not** be left unattended anywhere in Algonquin Park except (by written authority from the Park Superintendent) on:*
Little Cauchon Lake at the Carl Wilson Lake portage; Little Cedar Lake at the entrance to Aura Lee Lake; Manitou Lake at the Three Mile and Shada Lake portages; North Tea Lake at the Manitou Lake portage; Opeongo Lake at the Happy Isle, Redrock, Proulx and Wright Lake portages; Rock Lake at the Pen and Louisa Lake portages; Smoke Lake at the Ragged Lake portage; and all marked portages off of Cedar, Grand, Kioshkokwi, Mangotasi and White Partridge.
All boats and canoes must be removed from the Park at the end of each trip.

9.2 Forest Management

All **forest management operations** are restricted in Algonquin Park to places, times and areas approved by the Ministry within the Recreation/Utilization Zone. All operations must conform to the *Environmental Assessment Act* and be carried out in accordance with Ministry implementation manuals. They must also subscribe to specific restrictions that protect Park values.

Overall, the Ministry is interested in protecting site quality, carrying out vegetation management, protecting wildlife and fisheries habitat, maintaining appropriate aesthetic and noise standards, and reducing conflicts with recreational use. The Ministry monitors all operations to ensure that restrictions are being adhered to on such things as timing and location.

9.2.1 Areas of Concern

The **area of concern** process within the Park Forest Management Plan is used to modify forest management operations and to protect Park values. This process of identifying natural, cultural or recreational values for protection results in the establishment of no-cut reserves and modified cutting areas. The width of the area of concern and the no-cut or modified cut areas varies depending on the particular value (e.g., waterbody, wildlife) and characteristics of the land base.

- In no-cut reserves, no marking or cutting is done within a minimum (slope dependent) of 30 metres of any body of water, 30 metres of a public road and railway rights-of-way, 60 metres of portages, winter portages, and ski trails, or 15 metres of the Algonquin Park boundary, except for recreation or aesthetic purposes.
- Modified cutting areas, which occur beyond the no-cut reservations, specify the type of silvicultural system used and the degree of cutting.
- All slash within 120 metres of publicly used waters, public roads, railway rights-of-way, portages and trails must have tops removed from the reserve or lopped to within 1 metre of the ground where safety permits.

A misty morning in Algonquin

9.2.2 Special Management Areas

Vegetation management is modified in **Special Management Areas** (SMAs). Classes I and II SMAs are designated to protect significant earth science features. Class I SMAs include sites that require special management strategies to maintain their earth science values (see Appendix G for details). Class II SMAs include sites that will require no additional protection measures because the earth science values are resistant to forest management activities. Within both classes of SMAs, the most significant (provincially significant) or sensitive features are designated Nature Reserve Zones (Spek, 1993).

9.2.3 Noise Standards

Noise standards are maintained by the Ministry, designating the timing and location of operations.

- Forest management operations (including road construction) carried out between the last Saturday in June and Labour Day (both dates inclusive) are prohibited within 1.6 kilometres of canoe routes and recreational trails.
- During this same period, the movement of hauling trucks and other heavy equipment to, from, and through these areas is restricted to between 7:30 a.m. and 6:30 p.m. daylight saving time (Monday to Friday inclusive, statutory holidays exclusive) with the exception of the Achray/Lake Travers Road and all roads north of the Petawawa River (see Appendix F).
- In harvest areas adjacent to high off-season recreational use areas or where the topography permits sound travel, noise restrictions may be adjusted in both the timing and distance of operations as determined at the Forest Management Planning Stage.

9.2.4 Location and Standards for Work Camps and Other Structures

The **location and standards for work camps and other structures** are also prescribed and authorized by the Ministry.

- Only temporary portable work camps for forestry purposes are permitted and are located out of sight and more than 0.8 kilometres from the shore of canoeable lakes and streams or from portages and hiking trails.
- A permanent work camp, presently located at Odenback, will be removed when the adjacent concentration

yard is relocated or no longer required. This situation will be reviewed at least every five years.

- Camp layout, location and sanitary facilities must have the Park Superintendent's advance approval.
- All structures will be removed after use and sites cleaned up by the AFA.
- Sawmills, new concentration yards and forest manufacturing facilities are prohibited in the Park.
- Existing concentration yards, which include Daventry, Lake Travers and Odenback, will be phased out once they are no longer required or when alternative locations outside the Park are established.
- The AFA will ensure that existing concentration yards within the Park will not exceed 5 hectares, that they will not be used after the long weekend in July and before Labour Day, and that all debris will be disposed of as fuelwood, burned, chipped, mulched or removed on a continuous basis. Portable chipping will be permitted but will be subject to sound zone restrictions. Site rehabilitation will be completed once the site has been abandoned.

9.2.5 Roads and Landings

The location of **roads and landings** is given special consideration.

- All landings will be restricted in size to a maximum of 0.2 hectares.
- All roads must be constructed in accordance with the Ministry's *Environmental Guidelines for Access Roads and Water Crossings*, as well as any additional road construction techniques prescribed to protect Park values.
- Roads are developed in accordance with the permanent forest management road system strategy and are contained within an approved Forest Management Plan.
- A long-term strategy for the development of tertiary roads will be produced based on wood flow. The specific location of tertiary roads will be pre-approved at the Annual Work Schedule Stage.
- Maximum road rights-of-way have been established for all types of roads, including primary (13.7 metres), secondary and tertiary (9.1 metres), as well as for roads crossing no-cut timber reserves (6.7 metres).
- All timber must be cut and salvaged from rights-of-way.
- No roads may be constructed within 120 metres of waters, portages, public roads, railway rights-of-way and the Park boundary, except in accordance with the strategy for roads crossing canoe routes (Appendix F).
- Existing roads will be used to gain access to previously cut harvest areas except where Park values will be compromised. Existing roads are roads that were used in the previous harvest.
- Roads or clearings will not be permitted within Nature Reserve, Historical or Wilderness Zones.
- Existing roads located in Nature Reserve or Historical Zones will be phased out where possible. Most of these roads were developed prior to the establishment of the Nature Reserve or Historical Zones.
- Existing roads in Wilderness Zones will be phased out.
- Existing roads in the Recreation/Utilization Zone may also be phased out if alternative means of access, which would have a lesser impact on Park values, are available or possible.
- Existing road crossings of the Park boundary, other than public access roads, may be phased out, and no new road crossings will be permitted.

9.2.6 Recreational Use of Logging Roads

The **recreational use of logging roads** demonstrates how recreation and forestry can exist to their mutual benefit. The primary use of these roads is for forest product extraction and Park management. The secondary uses of some of these roads may be for recreational activities, such as dogsledding, horseback riding, mountain biking or other similar activities. However, the forest industry and the Park will recognize, in their planning, the requirements of recreational operators for business planning and trail preparation.

- Recreational activities on logging roads will be separated in time and space from forest management operations. In the event of a conflict, the recreational uses will be directed to other areas.
- The Ministry, the AFA and the recreational operators will address ecological, forestry and recreational concerns in their advance planning.
- Trail locations may vary from year to year. Through information and proper signage, the location of trails will be made clear each operating season to ensure visitor safety.

9.2.7 Road Crossings of Waterways and Portages

Road crossings of waterways and portages are limited to those essential for timber harvesting activities and are subject to other resource protection considerations. Where such crossings are necessary, the protection of fisheries habitat and the maintenance of water quality are provided for through the application of environmental guidelines, such as the Ministry's *Environmental Guidelines for Access Roads and Water Crossings*, *Code of Practice for Timber Management Operations in Riparian Areas*, and *Timber Management Guidelines for the Protection of Fish Habitat*. In addition, district approval procedures, mitigative techniques and methods of avoiding critical habitats are used.

- Road crossings of canoe routes are by bridge, with a clearance to preclude the need for portaging.
- Roads between 120 and 460 metres of canoe routes have a right-of-way width of 9.1 metres.
- Waterway and portage crossings by roads will be constructed in accordance with the strategy for roads that cross canoe routes (Appendix F).
- Crossings may be temporary or permanent.

- No new crossings of portages or canoe routes will be allowed unless no other options are available. The trading of one crossing for another is not allowed.
- An existing crossing may be eliminated if its existence is no longer justified.
- Sections of roads that cross portages, trails and navigable or publicly used streams and rivers will be rehabilitated after use to hasten the return of vegetation, thereby minimizing the impact on the recreational use of the Interior and ensuring greater site protection.

9.2.8 Transportation of Timber and Other Activities

Transportation of timber harvested in the Park is via the Park's road network to forest products industries located outside the Park.

- The rafting of logs across lakes and the driving of rivers is prohibited in the Park, and Park waters may not be used as log storage areas.
- The transportation of unmanufactured forest products from areas outside Algonquin Park to manufacturing facilities outside via Algonquin roads is permitted only over public roads in the Park.
- The **salvage** of old logs from Algonquin Park waters is not permitted.
- **Herbicides** may be used in commercial vegetation control in the Recreation/Utilization Zones; however, the AFA will look at viable alternatives to the use of herbicides for silvicultural purposes. Herbicides will only be used as a last resort.
- **Aggregate** pit use and operation will be carried out as described in Section 8.1.3.

9.3 Compliance Monitoring and Enforcement

The enforcement of regulations is part of resource and recreation management. As an operational program, it consists of three parts: education, information and enforcement. The management of Algonquin Park is heavily dependent upon visitor education as well as regulations and guidelines designed to protect the Park's natural resources and the quality of a visitor's recreational experience. Personal contacts and printed material are used to disseminate information. Public education and the presence of staff can mitigate the need for further restrictions and reduce the number of charges.

Enforcement is carried out for all **resource management activities** in the Park. The Park's lands and waters are protected under legislation and through special management guidelines outlined in this plan. Leaseholders must comply with such regulations as the *Lakes and Rivers Improvement Act*, *Public Lands Act* and *Environmental Protection Act,* and with the conditions of their lease. Forest management activities are monitored by both Ministry staff and the AFA to ensure that work is conducted in accordance with the *Crown Forest Sustainability Act* and other applicable acts, regulations and Park guidelines. Fire officers as well as conservation officers and park wardens enforce the *Forest Fire Prevention Act* and carry out inspections to see that the conditions of work permits have been met.

Recreation management also relies on enforcement activities. The *Provincial Parks Act* and its regulations are enforced by conservation officers, deputy conservation officers and park wardens. Algonquin Park officers also enforce up to 16 other provincial statutes including the *Game and Fish Act*, *Liquor Licence Act*, *Fisheries Act* and regulations under them.

- Regulatory controls are introduced or modified as required.
- Officers also provide some assistance to other operational or management programs, such as the animal control program.
- Personal contact is an effective means of delivering enforcement and public education messages, but Park signage and publications (e.g., tabloids and canoe route maps) are also essential in relaying important regulatory messages and to further educate the public in recreation management problems. In campgrounds, the information covers noise and liquor-related offences while Interior information emphasizes regulations governing campfire use, can and bottle ban, fishing limits and the cutting of live vegetation. Future changes in management policies may occur to facilitate recreation management.

The **Ontario Provincial Police** (OPP), who have a mandate for enforcement within the Provincial Parks System, have eight OPP detachments that have jurisdiction in Algonquin Park. The OPP are responsible for criminal, and search and rescue procedures and MNR staff assist the OPP as required. The Whitney OPP detachment routinely patrols the Parkway Corridor Development Zone with a special emphasis on criminal investigations, *Highway Traffic Act* violations and boating regulations.

9.4 Natural Heritage Education

Natural Heritage Education encompasses all aspects of the Park's operations: fish, wildlife, fire, forestry and recreation. It provides Park visitors with information and programs that foster their appreciation of Park natural and cultural values.

The Natural Heritage Education Program is designed to provide information, interpretation and recreational skills development to visitors. The Park Natural Heritage Education Program is the largest program of its kind in the provincial parks system, making approximately one million contacts per year through its facilities, publications and personal contacts.

The program is enhanced and product development is facilitated through an agreement between the Park and its co-operating association, the **Friends of Algonquin Park**. This agreement includes an array of Park publications and the operation of two bookstores.

The Natural Heritage Education Program is developed and presented in concert with other Park programs. Fisheries, wildlife and forestry personnel provide technical and professional expertise and assist in the development and presentation of Natural Heritage Education initiatives.

A Natural Heritage Education Plan has been completed. It outlines the facilities, programs and services that make up the Natural Heritage Education Program and indicates future strategies or initiatives. This plan has been developed in accordance with the provincial and regional Natural Heritage Education policies and strategies and will be updated to reflect new Park strategies. It will also be revised to reflect new facilities and the enhanced role of the Friends of Algonquin Park in delivering the program (see Strickland et al., 1981).

The Park's Natural Heritage Education Program is classified as a "major activity" program. Operating out of the Visitor Centre, it provides all three components of the program year-round: information, interpretation and recreational skills development. The program will also serve as a resource centre for programs in nearby parks.

9.4.1 Information

Visitors to Algonquin Park require information on the Park's facilities, activities, services, rules and regulations, management, recreational opportunities, and unique attractions. Information is provided outside the Park through personal contacts and the distribution of publications to media, interest groups, peripheral provincial parks and the provincial parks system information service at Queen's Park, as well as to outside travel and tourism-oriented agencies (see Section 9.5, Marketing and Tourism).

Within Algonquin Park, the Natural Heritage Education Program supplies information through facilities, programs, and personal contacts, as well as the use of print, audio-visual and display media and signs.

Information is conveyed through 27 different **facilities** in the Park including: the East and West Gates on Highway 60, a reservation office, 5 campground offices, 13 access points and 2 store/outfitting concessions, as well as the Visitor Centre and the Logging Museum (see Section 10.4).

Visitors also receive information through **personal contacts** with Park staff and private contractors or through special group visits with park wardens, conservation officers, Interior crews, AFA or other Ministry staff in the Park. Park staff include reservations, park operations, resource management, enforcement and Natural Heritage Education personnel. Reservations staff provide personal or written information to those planning to visit the Park. Staff operating the East and West Gate Information Centres and permit-issuing stations (campground offices and access points) provide information verbally as well as through the distribution of publications. Natural Heritage Education staff provide information at interpretive facilities, such as the Visitor Centre and Logging Museum, and through interpretive programs, such as conducted hikes, audio-visual shows and campsite visitations. Limited services in French are available from staff in the Park.

Park **publications** are an essential means of information delivery in the Park and currently consist of more than 50 publications, including the Park leaflet, Highway 60 and Interior tabloids, campground brochures, winter trails information, maps, and the Park's newsletter *The Raven*. Almost all of these publications are available in French, and some have been translated into other languages.

Signs located in the Park also serve to identify facilities, direct visitors and provide information on the Park's resources or management policies and are part of a comprehensive **Sign Plan**.

- A short-range radio station has been established to broadcast Park information and upcoming events.

9.4.2 Interpretation

Algonquin Park contains a very rich cross-section of both natural and cultural resources which can be effectively interpreted. Through the Natural Heritage Education interpretive program, visitors gain a better understanding, appreciation, and enjoyment of the Park. The interpretive program is available in many areas of the Park but is primarily focused on those areas that have large concentrations of visitors. It caters to all user groups and is organized on the basis of visitor activity preferences and themes associated with Algonquin Park's character, history and natural qualities.

Great Blue Heron

The major Algonquin interpretive themes include: geology and geomorphology, flora and fauna, human history and the Algonquin wilderness. Interpretation is carried out through the use of facilities, self-use or guided activities and programs.

The interpretive program uses the Visitor Centre and the Logging Museum to present audio-visual programs, natural and cultural exhibits and interpretive programs or events. The former Park museum has been redeveloped and is now the Algonquin Gallery.

In summer there are daily interpretive **programs** and events conducted in other areas of the Park, including slide presentations at the Pog Lake Outdoor Theatre and guided walks along trails. Children's programs, special events such as wolf howls and individual group presentations are also carried out in different areas of the Park. These programs are scheduled on a regular basis during the peak season but are reduced during the off-season. Personal contact between visitors services staff and Park visitors at the Visitor Centre and Logging Museum also offer opportunities for interpretation. A great deal of interpretive information is also provided through Park **publications**. Interpretive publications include trail guides, weekly editions of the Park newsletter (*The Raven*), a canoe route map (containing both practical and interpretive material), technical bulletins and books on the natural and cultural features of the Park.

- The interpretive program will continue to expand with the addition of **new** events, programs and publications as well as facilities.
- Greater emphasis will also be placed on delivering a Natural Heritage Education Program on the north and east sides of the Park (Achray, Brent and Kiosk), through self-guided trails, guidebooks and signs.

9.4.3 Recreation

Recreation is a component of the Natural Heritage Education Program that is directed toward developing visitors' outdoor recreational skills so that they may enjoy the Park. Recreational skills development in Algonquin emphasizes the more popular recreational activities, such as canoeing and camping, but also focuses on other interests, such as fishing and bird watching. These skills are taught through slide and film presentations, conducted hikes, special events (canoe demonstrations) and publications (such as the canoe route map) that contain practical information on canoeing and camping.

Park staff, contractors and volunteers have a major role in skills development through personal contacts with visitors.

9.5 Marketing and Tourism

Marketing in Algonquin is a management tool that identifies the characteristics of visitors and their needs. It also communicates with these groups how the Park can meet their needs.

Algonquin Park attracts **visitors** from all over the world. The majority (85%) of visitors originate from the immediate vicinity of the Park and southern Ontario, and the remainder from outside the province. Provincial user surveys have also determined that two-thirds of Park visitors are small groups of two to four people, with couples and small families predominating. Visitors to Algonquin may also be classified according to whether they are day users, car campers or Interior users and by their principal activities while in the Park, such as canoeing, camping, fishing, picnicking, sightseeing, cross-country skiing and hiking. These visitor patterns and statistics are useful for monitoring user trends to determine marketing strategies.

- A **marketing plan** will be produced to describe how the Park will be marketed in relation to specific user groups. It will be produced in concert with the Algonquin Park Management Plan, the Park Marketing Study, the Provincial Parks Marketing Plan, the Ministry of Economic Development, Trade and Tourism marketing plans and the marketing plans of the Chambers of Commerce, tourist associations and travel associations in the area.

Currently, marketing of Algonquin Park is achieved through the use of publications, media, travel and trade shows, and familiarization tours. This involves providing accurate and timely information through television, radio, newspapers, signs, magazines, maps, travel guides and booklets.

Distribution or use of this marketing material or expanding existing markets is also facilitated by communicating with the private sector, special interest groups, other Ministries (in particular the Ministry of Citizenship, Culture and

Recreation and the Ministry of Transportation), tourist associations, travel associations and local Chambers of Commerce.

Private enterprises such as resorts, outfitters and clubs/ organizations located inside and outside the Park promote their services in relation to the Park, and thus indirectly promote Algonquin.

As part of their tourism-oriented services, the Chambers of Commerce, tourist associations and travel associations adjacent to the Park provide information on Algonquin to travellers.

The Ministry of Citizenship, Culture and Recreation assists in marketing and promoting Algonquin as part of its own provincial mandate, through its international travel trade offices around the world, travel information centres across the province, regional field offices and telecommunication centre in Toronto. Its advertising and promotion section also provides coverage of Algonquin in its maps, guides and booklets. The Ministry of Transportation assists by incorporating information on Algonquin into the Official Road Map of Ontario and by providing external highway signs.

- **Future** marketing strategies may incorporate new activities, programs, services and facilities to meet visitors' needs and attract new visitors both nationally and internationally.
- Activities in the shoulder seasons and in under-utilized areas will also be examined.
- A specific clientele will be targeted for new and renovated facilities and services that were put in place for the 100th anniversary of Algonquin, including the new Visitor Centre and the Logging Museum.
- More innovative techniques for providing timely and accurate information to an anticipated increase in the volume and diversity of visitors will be considered.
- Concessions and outfitting services that provide essential supplies and services to visitors will also continue to be upgraded.

9.6 Research

Algonquin has a long history of encouraging field-oriented research and more than 1,800 scientific papers have been published on research activities in the Park. Typically, more than two dozen research programs are conducted annually in the fields of biology, geology, human history and user behaviour. Some projects are short-term while others span years or even decades. This research has contributed to the knowledge of the Park's natural and cultural history, to its resource and recreational management as well as the Park's interpretive program.

The Park provides numerous opportunities for research because of its unique location, large area, relatively natural conditions, diversity of flora and fauna and research facilities. Four research facilities exist in the Park and are used extensively by the Ministry and the academic community.

- Since 1944 the Wildlife Research Station at Sasajewun Lake has carried out considerable work on mammals, birds and invertebrates.
- The Forest Research Station at Swan Lake conducts long-term ecological research that is essential for sustainable ecosystem management.
- The Harkness Laboratory of Fisheries Research on Lake Opeongo was established in 1936 to study lake productivity and the dynamics of fish populations and communities (with an emphasis on Lake Trout, Brook Trout and Smallmouth Bass).
- In 1976 the Algonquin Fisheries Assessment Unit was established as part of a provincial network to collect information on a series of 'type lakes' to assist staff in managing the fishery both in the Park and in similar type lakes across the province. The lakes monitored in the Park are representative of cold, deep waterbodies with fish communities consisting of self-sustaining populations of Lake and Brook Trout and Smallmouth Bass. The long-term monitoring program examines the effects of stresses such as acid rain and exploitation, and evaluates various management actions in the Park.
- Many other research programs are carried out in the Park without the benefit of research facilities. These may include field studies such as recreational surveys or acid rain monitoring.

The Algonquin Park Visitor Centre, while not a research facility, plays an important role in facilitating Park research by maintaining historical and photographic **archives** and important botanical, zoological, geological and archaeological collections that are available for use by the research community. A list of current Park research projects is maintained at the Visitor Centre, and copies of all reports, scientific papers, theses and books are housed in the library.

One additional research facility, the Algonquin Radio Observatory, is operated at Lake Travers by Natural Resources Canada. The Observatory and its research activities are dependent on the stable geological conditions at this location on the Canadian Shield. Recently, the purpose and scale of the research program and its support facilities have been completely reviewed and the focus narrowed to the needs of global and planetary navigation. This has identified the future need for only the large radio dish and a small amount of the existing facility infrastructure.

All **research programs** require the approval of the Park Superintendent and must meet all the requirements under applicable provincial and federal legislation.

- A Research Management Plan will be developed for the Park by an interdisciplinary Park Research Committee.
- Research activities and facilities must be compatible with protection objectives and recreational uses in the Park.
- Research activities are subject to development and management policies for Natural Environment Parks unless otherwise permitted.
- Removal of natural materials or artifacts is strictly prohibited unless authorized by the Park Superintendent, and any materials removed remain the property of the Ministry.
- Sites altered by research activities will be rehabilitated to as close to their original condition as possible.
- Research proposals may originate from within or outside the Ministry of Natural Resources; however, the Ministry will encourage outside researchers to address specific questions of concern to Park resource management.
- Research activities will be consistent with the Ontario Parks Research and Information Strategy (1997) and Park Management Policy P.M. 2.45.
- Research proposals are evaluated by the Park Research Committee (and outside authorities as required) based on the principle that the potential benefits of the research must outweigh the impact of the research on Park users and resources. Only if the positive benefits of the research outweigh any negative impacts is permission granted. Otherwise, modifications may be required or the project proposal is denied. This ensures that there will be no unacceptable impact on either the environment or the use of the area, and that the collection or destruction of any materials will be strictly controlled.

10.0 Development Policies

Structures and improvements in Algonquin Park are limited to those needed to support the level of services to Park visitors described in this plan. These facilities are located primarily in Development and Access Zones and to a lesser degree in Wilderness, Natural Environment and Recreation/ Utilization Zones.

- The extent and nature of future development will be limited by the carrying capacity of the Park itself.
- New developments or improvements to existing structures are carried out in accordance with the Provincial Parks Development Standards and Development Policies, as well as approved site and development plans.
- All development projects must conform to the *Environmental Protection Act* and be approved under the *Environmental Assessment Act.*
- All new recreational facilities and improvements to existing facilities will provide barrier-free access to the physically challenged, where possible.

Proposed future development projects or improvements will be contingent upon available funding (see Section 11.0, Implementation). These facilities (**Figure 4**), both existing and future, are described under the following categories: recreation, access and circulation, commercial, Natural Heritage Education, research, administrative and operational facilities, and utilities.

10.1 Recreational Facilities

A variety of structures and improvements have been developed to provide recreational facilities and services in Algonquin Park. The majority of development has occurred at the beaches and lakes of the Parkway Corridor or at access points around the perimeter of the Park. In the Parkway Corridor Development Zone and some peripheral Development Zones (e.g., Kiosk, Brent and Achray), campgrounds, day use areas and/or interpretive facilities have been developed to support the greatest concentrations of visitors. In comparison, minimal development has been required in the Wilderness, Natural Environment and Recreation/Utilization Zones to sustain Interior use.

- Future recreational developments and improvements will be designed to provide for a greater variety of activities, improve the quality of services and facilities and realign these facilities and services to ensure their support of the Park goal and objectives.
- There will be minimal provision of facilities to accommodate additional campers and trippers in the Parkway Corridor.
- Any development will be focused on the perimeter areas, and further study will be undertaken to determine their needs.

Existing and future recreational facility developments in the Park are described under the following headings: day use, Development Zone camping and Interior camping.

10.1.1 Day Use Facilities

Day use facilities allow visitors to participate in such activities as hiking, bicycling, cross-country skiing, scenic/ wildlife viewing, picnicking, fishing, canoeing, horseback riding, dogsledding, hunting, snowshoeing and visiting Park interpretive facilities while also experiencing the natural, scientific and historical aspects of the Park.

The majority of day users participate in activities using facilities along the Parkway Corridor, while a smaller number go into the Interior through various access points around the periphery of the Park. The opportunities to gain an initial appreciation of Algonquin through day visits will be enhanced as a greater variety of day use facilities and services are provided or existing ones improved.

Day use trails operated in the Park include interpretive, cross-country ski, bicycle, horseback riding, dogsled and snowshoe.

- Some trails may be used for different seasonal uses.
- Summer horseback riding opportunities are available on the Leaf Lake ski trail system, on logging roads in the McManus Lake area near Achray and in Clyde and Bruton Townships, when these roads are not being used for logging.
- The horseback riding, dogsled and snowshoe trails may also be used for camping.
- Cross-country skiing and snowshoeing are not limited to designated travel routes.
- The development, maintenance and operation of recreational trails in Algonquin Park by the private sector may be permitted but must be authorized in advance, by the Park Superintendent (e.g., horseback riding trails of youth camps and Algonquin Nordic Ski Trails in Bruton Township).
- Trail development and use must have minimal impact on the Park's environment and other users.
- The continued operation of new types of trail facilities depends on level of use, funding or the establishment of co-operative management agreements with clubs or associations interested in maintaining the trails.

- Concession services will continue to offer equipment rentals for a variety of seasonal activities.

  (See Section 9.2.6, Recreational Use of Logging Roads.)

Wildlife/scenic viewing opportunities are available along the Parkway Corridor.
- Wildlife/scenic viewing opportunities may be improved through the provision of viewing areas in Development, Recreation/Utilization and Natural Environment Zones.

A scenic view

Picnic areas have been established along the Parkway Corridor (Highway 60). Since bathing opportunities are available at only three of these facilities, demand presently exceeds supply.
- Although further opportunities are limited by the present level of development on lakes in the Corridor, day use opportunities for picnicking and swimming can be increased by upgrading existing sites and creating a few new sites along the Parkway Corridor or on the Park periphery.

Most waterways in the Park, with the exception of fish sanctuaries, offer **fishing** opportunities.
- Further opportunities for shore fishing in day use areas, especially for families and people with disabilities, will be pursued.

Interpretive facilities include the Visitor Centre and the Logging Museum. The former Park Museum has been converted into the Algonquin Gallery (see Section 10.4, Natural Heritage Education Facilities).

10.1.2 Campground Facilities

Campground facilities include car campgrounds as well as walk-in and paddle-in campsites.

In the **Parkway Corridor Development Zone**, there are currently 1,220 campsites in eight campgrounds, 16 paddle-in campsites and a group camping facility with 18 sites.
- Future development or expansion of facilities along the Parkway Corridor will be limited to avoid infringing on other users, the Interior and Park values.
- All campgrounds in the Parkway Corridor Development Zone will be maintained at, or close to, their present levels. Development will emphasize the upgrading and rehabilitation of existing campgrounds and sites and the redevelopment of sites to replace site closures.
- Existing campgrounds will also be improved through the provision of new or renovated facilities, including washrooms, showers, electrical sites and other site amenities.
- Additional paddle-in, walk-in or boat-in sites may be provided to meet the demand for more secluded camping opportunities in proximity to campground areas.
- In total, approximately 1,350 campsites may be provided along the Parkway Corridor Development Zone. This limit reflects land capability, quality of visitor experience and public recommendations that further intensive development within the Park be limited and that additional demands be focused on perimeter areas.
- Limited winter camping opportunities will be provided, including car camping and more remote snowshoe and ski-in opportunities using existing facilities. The total number of sites operated and their locations will be based on need.

The **Kiosk, Brent** and **Achray Development Zones** located on the west, north and east peripheries of the Park contain approximately 84 sites within three campgrounds. These sites accommodate about 17,000 camper days of recreation per year.
- In these areas, future development of organized car campgrounds will be restricted to smaller, more intimate units.
- Roofed accommodation may be made available.
- The remaining access points will be upgraded where required and may be reviewed for campground development.
- The campground at **Kiosk**, located on the north side of the Park, currently provides 17 campsites. This campground may be redesigned and upgraded to park standards to provide additional campsites and to increase spacing between sites.
- The **Brent** campground contains 28 sites and may be redesigned to increase site capacity and to meet Park standards.

Figure 4 — Development

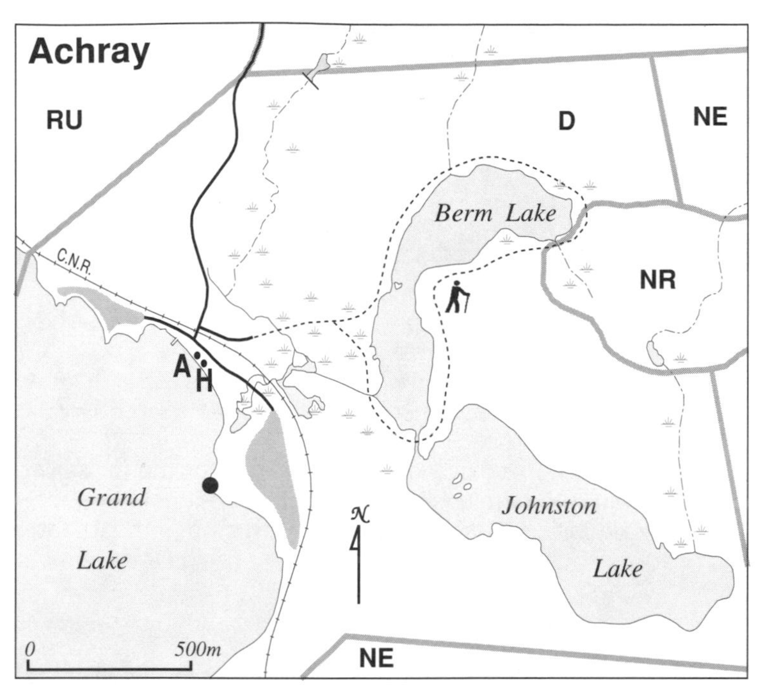

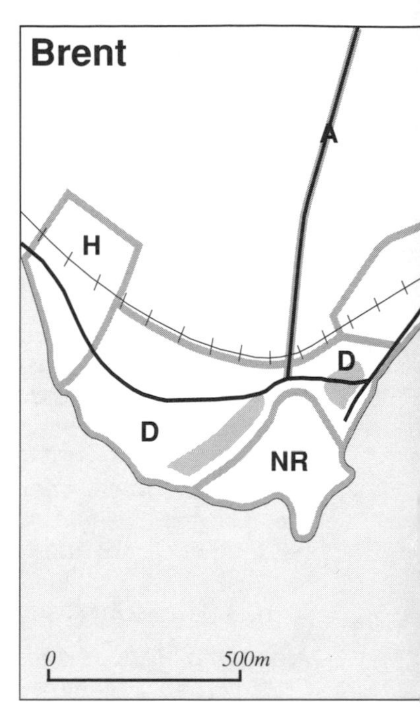

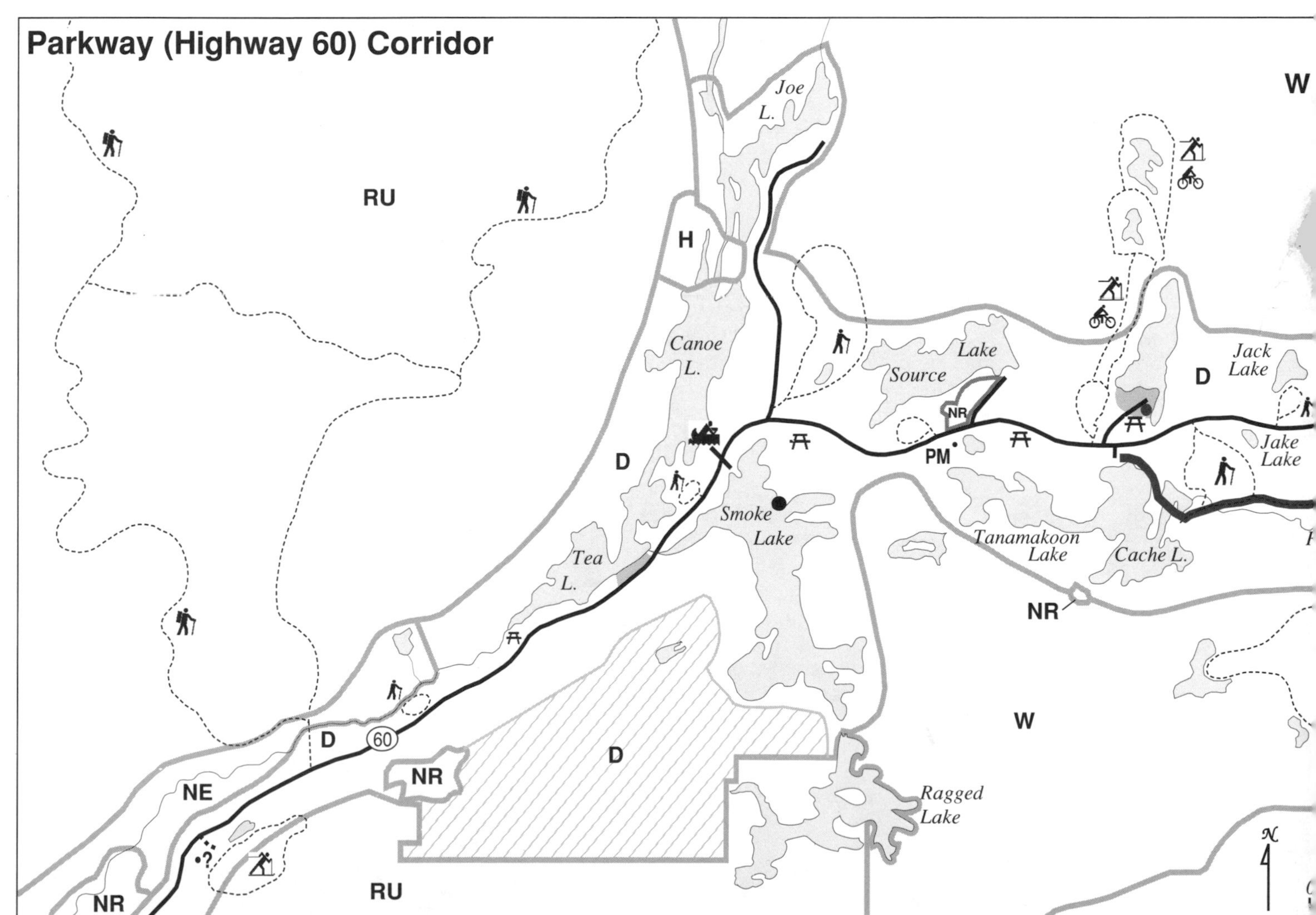

- Additional car camping opportunities may be provided on the east side of the Park. Other recreational opportunities such as a hiking trail or walk-in or paddle-in sites may also be provided there.

The **Rain Lake** access point, on the west side, contains 10 campsites and may be upgraded. The access point cabin is also available under the cabin rental program.

At **Basin Lake**, current facilities and services appear to be adequate. However, additional development may be considered if a need is demonstrated in the future.

The potential for campsite development, at the south end of the Park, at the **Kingscote Lake Access Point,** will be studied.

The rest of the car-oriented camping pressure on Algonquin Park will be met outside the Park in other provincial park, private park and resort area developments.

10.1.3 Interior Camping Facilities

Algonquin Park is the largest canoe-camping park in Ontario, and while it may not represent a true wilderness area, it does provide a high-quality experience for Interior travellers. Interior camping facilities include campsites for canoeists, backpackers, horseback riders, skiers, dogsledders and snowshoers.

The Interior of the Park currently generates about 300,000 camper days per annum through 1,946 Interior campsites located on a network of **canoe routes**. Access is gained to the Interior through nine access points along Highway 60 and through 20 access points on the perimeter of the Park (see Section 10.2, Access and Circulation).

Interior canoe-campsite development will be maintained at, or close to, current levels. Further campsite and canoe route development cannot be provided without a deterioration of canoe-camping or environmental quality. However, sites may be developed to replace those closed due to fire or overuse, and to allow for the redistribution of use patterns.

- User trends indicate that more canoeists are travelling to a particular destination area to camp. Therefore, additional sites may be developed within the first day's travel zone to accommodate both the destination campers and Interior trippers.
- Interior campsites will continue to be permitted in Nature Reserve Zones where they will not impair the values for which the zones were established. These campsites will be recognized as non-conforming uses within these zones. Portages, trails and signs for route identification will be provided where required.
- Additional improvements in facilities, such as upgrading access roads and access points, and increased campsite and canoe route maintenance will be undertaken as funding permits.

Existing ranger **cabins**, scattered throughout the Park, have been upgraded to preserve their heritage and to provide overnight accommodation for Interior users in all seasons. There are 14 cabins strategically located throughout the Interior that required only minor upgrading to meet public safety and fire protection standards. Some are accessible by canoe and some by road.

- The cabins are available for a fee and may be reserved through the Park reservation service.
- Cabins are equipped with bunks, a wood stove, a table, benches and other small accessories as required to retain their rustic character.
- Interior access point offices are responsible for selling permits, controlling use, upgrading and maintenance.
- No additional cabins will be constructed in the Interior. Any additional cabins will be built only in Development Zones where public access already exists.

McKaskill Lake cabin

Algonquin Park offers overnight camping opportunities on three long-distance **backpacking trails**. The 35-kilometre Highland Trail has 21 campsites and the Western Uplands Trail has 68 campsites along its 93-kilometre length. Both trails are accessible from the Parkway Corridor. Access to the top end of the latter trail can also be gained from the Rain Lake access point. The Eastern Pines Trail near Achray has two loops of 6 kilometres and 15 kilometres in length, with 14 Interior campsites.

- The need for and possible locations for the provision of additional backpacking opportunities on the east side of Algonquin Park will be considered.
- Further horseback riding opportunities with overnight camping facilities may be provided.

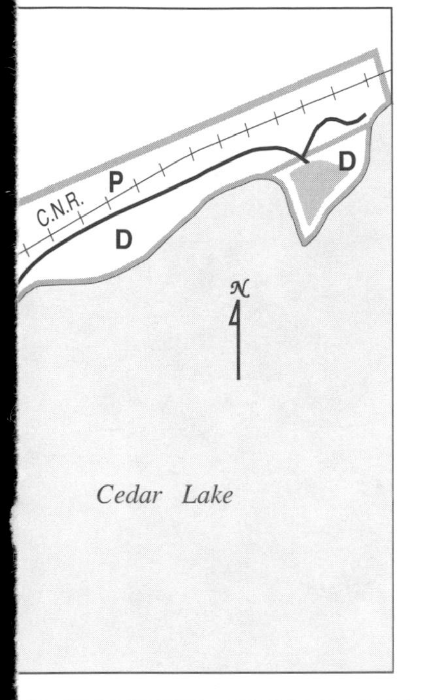

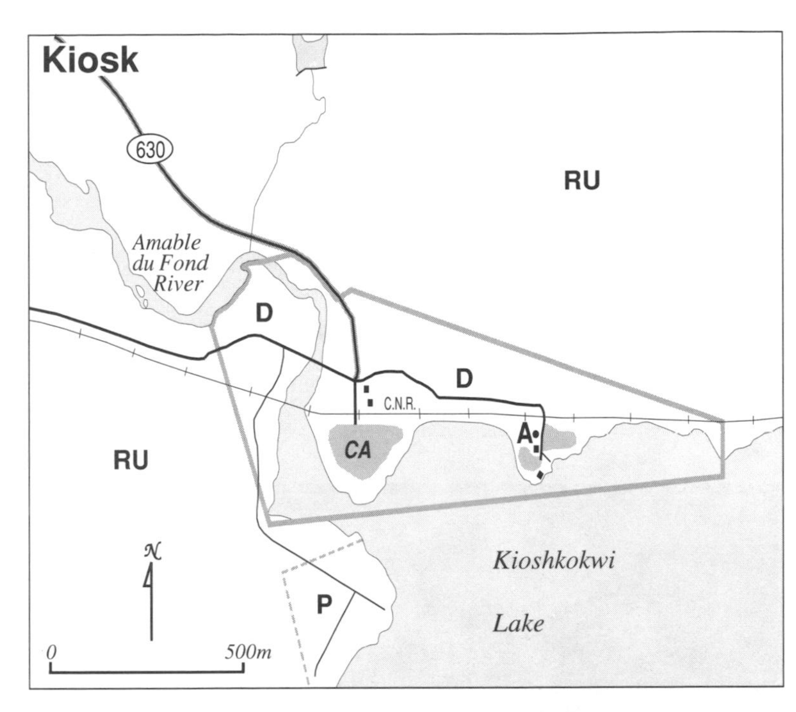

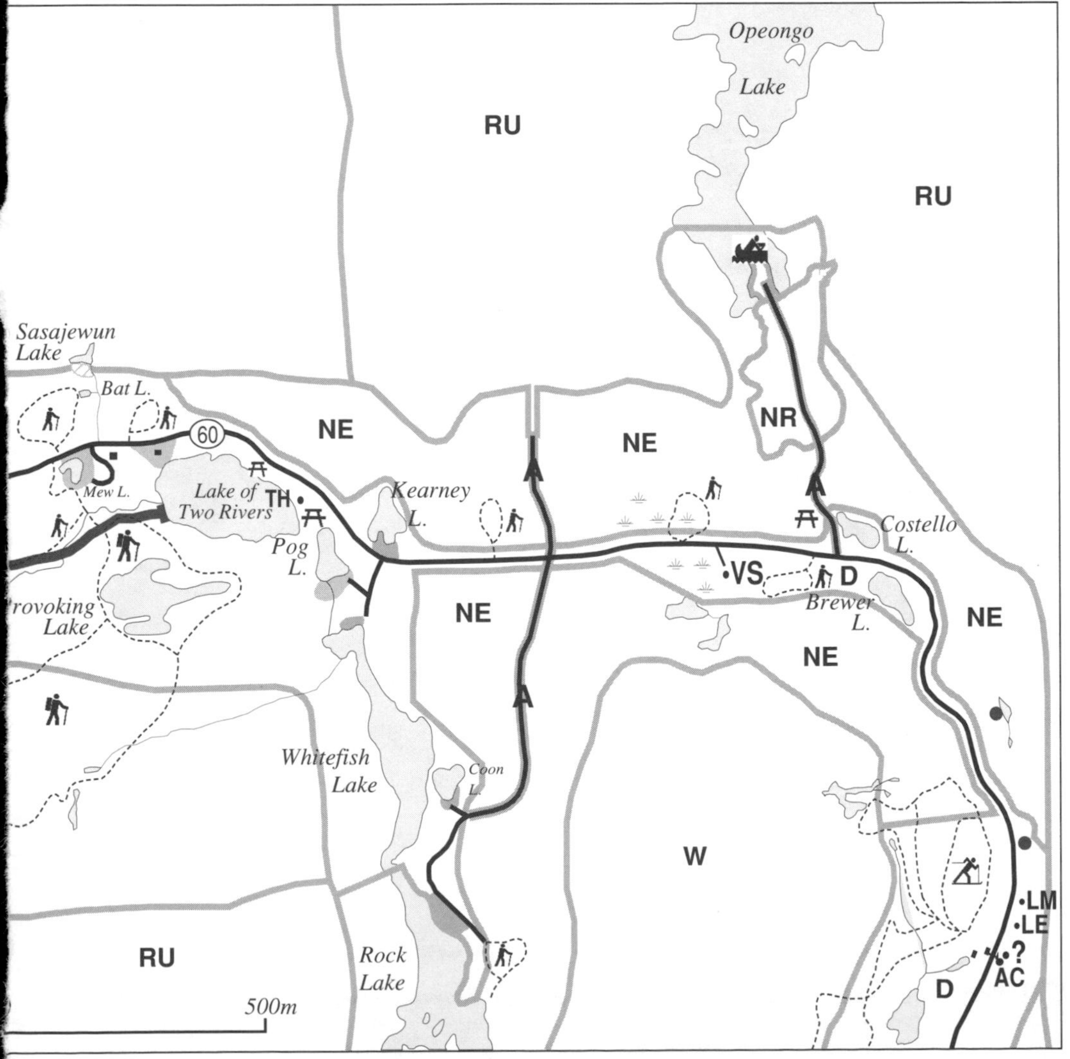

Legend

- **NR** Nature Reserve Zone
- **W** Wilderness Zone
- **NE** Natural Environment Zone
- **H** or ■ Historic Zone
- **D** Development Zone
- **A** Access Zone
- **RU** Recreation/Utilization Zone
- **P** Patented Land
- Day Use Trail
- Back-packing Trail
- Cross-country Ski
- Bicycle Trail
- Canoe Centre
- Picnic Grounds
- Campgrounds/Group Camping
- Access Road
- Research Area
- **•A** Access Point/Campground Office
- **•H** Historic Cabin
- **•TH** Outdoor Theatre
- **•PM** Park Museum (•S = Arts & Skills Centre
- **•?** Information Centre
- **•VS** Visitor Centre
- **•LM** Logging Museum
- **•LE** Logging Exhibit
- **•AC** Administrative Centre
- Campground Additions

Sight-seeing at the Barron Canyon

Cross-country skiing

Shooting rapids

- **Winter camping** must take place no closer than 30 metres from lakes, portages and Interior summer campsites.
- Temporary winter tent camps have been operated by commercial dogsledders for the benefit of their clients on a trial basis under agreement with the Park. These agreements will continue to be issued on a yearly basis and are limited to the organizations that have developed and are maintaining the dogsled trail for public use and for use by other commercial dogsledders.

10.2 Access and Circulation Facilities

Access routes provide a valuable means of designing, controlling and dispersing use in Algonquin Park. Access and circulation facilities consist of access points, roads and structures.

There are 29 **access points** and six **departure points** located around the perimeter of Algonquin. Highway 60, managed and operated by the Ministry of Transportation, is the main access road into the Park. This highway provides access to day use facilities, campgrounds and campground offices, interpretive facilities and nine locations for Interior access. The 20 other access points are located on the outer boundaries of the Park, and four of these access points also provide access to small developed campgrounds. Departure points are available on six rivers, four of which connect with the four waterway parks that border the Park.

- There will be no additional Interior access points developed other than a possible southern entry considered for the area of the Galipo Lakes.
- The upgrading (e.g., Brent Lake and Rain Lake access roads) or relocation of existing access roads and access points (e.g., Lake Travers and Shall Lake) is permitted.

There are two **provincial highways** within the Park, Highway 60 and 630. Highway 60 runs east-west through the lower third of the Park, with information centres located at the East and West Gates. At the information centres, Park visitors may purchase permits or receive information while traffic passing through the Park may proceed without delay. Highway 630, which extends 28 kilometres southward from Highway 17 into the former Kiosk townsite, provides access to the Kiosk Development Zone.

- There will be no additional highways routed in or through the Park and the widening of existing highways will be discouraged. However, minor re-alignments may be considered to improve traffic and visitor safety, provided Park values are not jeopardized.
- Modifications, such as additional turn-off lanes and pull-off areas, may be constructed on Highway 60 to provide viewing opportunities and to facilitate traffic flow.

Public park roads are constructed in Development and Access Zones to provide access to waterways and campgrounds located on the perimeter of the Park and along the Parkway.

Non-public park roads are restricted to authorized vehicles and are signed and/or gated accordingly. These roads are constructed and maintained by the AFA and MNR for forestry and park management activities in the Recreation/Utilization Zone, and are developed in accordance with the Park Management Plan and the Algonquin Park Forest Management Plan. All roads are designed and located to protect natural values and to minimize adverse effects on recreational resources.

- Roads are not permitted in Wilderness Zones.
- Where possible, roads located in Nature Reserve and Historical Zones will be phased out. Some of these were developed prior to the establishment of the zones.
- No new roads will be constructed in Nature Reserve or Historical Zones.
- Waterway and portage crossings by roads will be constructed in accordance with the strategy for roads that cross canoe routes (Appendix F).
- No new crossings of portages or canoe routes will be allowed unless no other options are available. This limits waterway and portage crossings by roads to the minimum essential for timber harvesting activities.
- The rationale for any existing crossings will be periodically reviewed, and crossings may be removed if their use is no longer justified.
- Existing road crossings of the Park boundary, other than public access roads, will be phased out where possible.
- No new road crossings of the boundary are permitted.
- As mentioned in Section 10.1, further trail development will be carried out to improve the recreational opportunities available for backpacking, dogsledding and horseback riding.
- The existing system of portages will be retained, but additional portages may be developed to inaccessible lakes for redistribution of use.
- Footbridges or boardwalks are provided only on trails and portages where users cannot safely use stepping stones or footlogs.
- Dock construction is limited to areas without suitable natural landings.
- Several canoe routes rely on the natural or artificial dams to sustain navigable water levels. Existing dams may be maintained or they may be removed, taking into consideration water levels essential for canoe travel as well as the impact on biota and aesthetics (see Section 8.2, Water Management).

10.3 Commercial Facilities

A number of commercial facilities are located in the Park that are operated by the private sector under commercial leases and agreements. These include lodges and youth camps, which have been privately developed, and Park-owned facilities that are operated by concessionaires.

The three lodges located along the Parkway Corridor provide accommodation and services to a segment of society that chooses not to camp but wish to partake of the Park environment. Lodge facilities include accommodation, dining, boat/canoe rentals, snack bars and recreational facilities.

The six youth camps located in the Corridor make a significant contribution to the park by increasing an awareness of natural areas among young people. Although the camps provide an array of on-site facilities for their programs, the primary focus of their programs is on environmental awareness through their tripping programs.

- All **privately owned facilities** in the Park are encouraged to pursue activities/programs that foster an understanding and appreciation of the natural environment and have a minimal impact on Park resources.
- They must receive prior authorization to develop new facilities or structures, or modify existing structures (with the exception of basic maintenance).
- Ontario Parks commenced to negotiate lease renewals in 1997 with all lodges and youth camps.
- The provision of additional moderately priced lodge services or hostels in the Park will be studied.

Commercial concessions operate in Park facilities under contract agreements to provide essential goods and services for visitors. These are provided to meet visitor needs rather than attempting to capitalize upon a business opportunity. Although in many instances visitor needs can be accommodated by facilities located outside of the Park, the distances involved in the Corridor make this impractical. Generally, the concession services and the locations where they are provided have an important impact on travel patterns and the quality of experience provided for all user groups. This principle and the definition of an acceptable, yet essential concession service are applied in drafting the concession proposals.

Currently there are concessions for firewood, laundry and outfitting services, stores and restaurants in the Park. The firewood and laundry concessions operate to service the campgrounds in the Parkway Corridor. Outfitting services at Canoe Lake, Opeongo Lake and Brent provide orientation and educational information to trippers as well as essential goods and services for visitors. Basic food and camping needs are also provided to the Interior campers at stores on Canoe and Opeongo Lakes, and a similar service is available to campground visitors at the Lake of Two Rivers Store. The Lake of Two Rivers Store, the Portage Store on Canoe Lake and the Visitor Centre also have restaurant facilities.

- Additional services may be provided where a need is identified, and with the approval of the Park Superintendent.
- The development of commercial facilities is not permitted on **patent land** located in the Park unless authorized by the Park Superintendent.

10.4 Natural Heritage Education Program Facilities

Natural Heritage Education facilities are located primarily along the Parkway Corridor in close proximity to the large concentrations of visitors. Information is made available at the East and West Gates, five campground offices, 9 access point offices, the Logging Museum and the Visitor Centre. Interpretive facilities include self-guided interpretive trails, the Tom Thomson Cabin, the Pog Lake Outdoor Theatre, the Visitor Centre and the Logging Museum.

There are 16 self-guided **interpretive trails**, 13 of which are located along the Parkway Corridor and three on the north and east sides of the Park. These trails, which are used by approximately 200,000 visitors per year, take advantage of scenic lookouts, vistas, historic sites and other special features. They provide outstanding hiking and viewing opportunities and interpret the natural and human history of the Park.

- Periodic reviews of user trends are conducted to determine the need for further interpretive opportunities.

Historic cabins in the Park include the Tom Thomson Cabin, which was used by the renowned artist who inspired the Group of Seven. Located at the Achray campground, the cabin has been restored to commemorate his life and work in Algonquin Park and to serve as an interpretive centre for the east side of the Park.

- Historic cabins located throughout the Park Interior (e.g., Cedar Lake) or at access points (e.g., Kiosk) will be upgraded to preserve their heritage value and may be used to provide overnight accommodation and interpretive opportunities.

The **Pog Lake Outdoor Theatre**, located midway along the Parkway Corridor, supports interpretive events that incorporate slide and film presentations.

The **Visitor Centre**, which replaced the Algonquin Park Museum in 1993, is an interpretive, library/archival and administrative facility for the Natural Heritage Education Program and the Friends of Algonquin Park. The 2,415-square metre Centre contains a large exhibit hall, theatre, bookstore, restaurant, meeting/ classroom, library, archives and associated offices and work areas. As an interpretive facility, it provides the visitor with the sights and sounds of Algonquin through displays that describe Algonquin's geology, climate, soils, forests, wildlife and history.

- Upgrading of the Visitor Centre building and exhibits will continue through support from the Ministry of Natural Resources, the Friends of Algonquin Park and private donations/sponsors.

The former Park Museum has been converted into the **Algonquin Gallery**.

The Algonquin **Logging Museum**, replacing the former Pioneer Logging Exhibit, was developed through the cooperative efforts of the Friends of Algonquin, the Ontario Ministry of Natural Resources and the Algonquin Forestry Authority. The Museum contains historical photos and carvings, a history-oriented bookstore and a theatre. The major exhibit is a sequence of exhibits laid out along a walking trail to describe the historic evolution of logging in the Park.

- Exhibits will continue to be added and enhanced.

10.5 Research Facilities

Research policies, programs and facilities are described in Section 9.6.

- No new research facilities are planned.
- Temporary facilities for approved research may be permitted where appropriate.
- The Algonquin Radio Observatory research program has been scaled down by Natural Resources Canada. The new focus on global navigation will continue into the foreseeable future. The future of any surplus facilities will be reviewed with respect to their usefulness for research and other Park needs.

10.6 Administrative and Operational Facilities

Administrative and operational facilities are required for daily operations in the Park and include the East and West Gate Complexes, the Visitor Centre, Summer Headquarters, the Achray and Kiosk work centres, 10 access point offices, five campground offices and the Clarke Lake and Smoke Lake Airbase.

The **East Gate Complex** consists of the Outdoor Recreation and Information Office, administrative offices, garage, central warehouse, Fisheries Assessment Unit office and seasonal staff accommodation. The complex provides work space, storage, distribution of materials and administrative support for all programs under the direction of the Park Superintendent.

- Future development projects for the East Gate Complex may include additional space for the Outdoor Recreation and Information Office, renovations to the central warehouse and the elimination of staff accommodations once alternative accommodations are available for seasonal staff near the Summer Headquarters.

Summer Headquarters is the main summer operational and maintenance facility for the Parkway Corridor. Buildings include a maintenance building, administrative office building, 40-person accommodations building and a dry storage building.

- Staff accommodation at Summer Headquarters will be enlarged and upgraded.

The **Visitor Centre** is the administrative and operational centre for the Natural Heritage Education Program and provides storage of historic and research documents. The facility contains the Natural Heritage Education staff and Friends of Algonquin staff, storage spaces, archives, displays, theatre and bookstore.

- The status of the seasonal staff residence adjacent to the Education Centre will be reviewed pending the final decision on development of staff accommodations in the Park.

Information centres, **campground offices** and **access points** located around the Park are specifically designed for information delivery and access control. East and West Gate Information Centres provide information to visitors entering the Park along the Parkway Corridor. Campground offices are located at Pog Lake, Mew Lake, Canisbay, Lake of Two Rivers and Rock Lake campgrounds within the Parkway Corridor Development Zone. There are 10 access point offices located in the Park, which, in conjunction with other private concessionaires located outside the Park, administer Interior use. Kiosk, Brent, Achray and Rain Lake also have small campgrounds.

- The Smoke Lake Airbase may be phased out once satisfactory alternative facilities are available elsewhere or the demand for air transport diminishes.

The Achray and Kiosk work centres are small, seasonal **administrative and operational centres**.

Achray Campground and Offices and the Sand Lake Gate provide administrative offices, access point office, maintenance equipment storage and staff accommodations for the Achray campground and Park Interior program on the east side.

The year-round operational headquarters for the Kiosk management area in the Park's northwest corner is at Samuel de Champlain Provincial Park, with a seasonal office, residence and campground located at Kiosk.

The Pembroke District Office also functions as an administrative centre for Algonquin Park. Park staff manage operations on the north and east sides of the Park from this facility, which also acts as a base for the two smaller administrative centres at Achray and Kiosk.

10.7 Utilities

The services or systems required to operate Algonquin Park are numerous. They include water, sanitation, sewage, waste removal (including recyclables), hydro, gasoline, propane and telephone systems. Each system has its own maintenance requirements and must meet provincial health, safety and environmental standards.

- The Park Superintendent must approve the location of any new systems or extensions to systems, including private services such as hydro and telephone distribution lines (the latter are underground wherever possible).
- Additional development of transmission lines is prohibited.
- There will be no new landfill sites permitted in the Park, and the existing landfill site at Achray has been eliminated.
- The transfer facility at Lake of Two Rivers will continue to handle refuse material, non-household waste and the storage of construction and recyclable materials.

Facility Development Summary

Recreation — general
- extent of facilities to be determined by the carrying capacity of the Park
- minimal new facilities to accommodate additional campers and trippers in the Parkway Corridor
- any new development to be focused on perimeter areas

Day Use
- new hiking, horseback, bicycling and dogsled trails possible

Campgrounds
- maintain drive-in campsites at or near existing levels along the Parkway Corridor
- some new paddle-in sites possible
- new drive-in sites possible at Kiosk, Brent and the east side

Interior
- maintain campsites at or near existing levels
- possible new destination sites near access points
- ranger cabins for roofed accommodation

Access/Circulation
- no new Interior access points, except possibly near the Galipo Lakes
- no new public roads

Private/Commercial Facilities
- may be developed as needed to provide essential goods and services
- study new medium-priced lodging facilities
- existing cottage leases to expire in 2017

Natural Heritage Education
- new interpretive trails possible

Research Facilities
- no new permanent facilities planned

11.0 Implementation

Algonquin Park has had a significant impact on the regional and provincial economies for over 100 years and that impact has grown and become well established over these years. The two major components of that impact are the recreation/tourism and forest industries.

11.1 Recreation/tourism Industry

The recreation/tourism industry impact of a provincial park normally includes the expenditures for public sector facility operations and capital development, and the spending by campers and day visitors. However, in Algonquin Park, there are also expenditures for private sector facility operations and capital development (e.g. concessions, lodges, youth camps and private cottages) and the spending by patrons of these facilities. Although not all of this spending can be easily identified and monitored, from what is known of public sector spending, it would appear to be substantial.

Indeed, 1996/97 expenditures by the public sector and their patrons in the Park* are indicative of the scale of impact that exists. Based on initial expenditures of approximately $29.8 million there was an estimated provincial impact of $75.9 million. Of this total $35.4 million was spent on wages and salaries creating 843 person years of provincial employment. Of this total, 446 person years occurred in the region, mostly within the Park itself.

If data were available for the private sector facilities noted above, these figures would likely be considerably higher.

11.2 Forest Industry

Although forest management is not permitted within the provincial park system it does occur in Algonquin Park as an 'exception' to provincial policy. The forest industry in the Park is controlled and operated by the Algonquin Forest Authority (AFA), a crown corporation which supplies forest products to manufacturing industries in the region and across southern Ontario. The economic impact from forest management within the park itself is associated with the planning, harvesting, renewal and maintenance of the forest resource based on an ecologically sustainable basis. There is also considerable economic activity associated with secondary processing and manufacturing of forest products in adjacent communities.

*Prepared by Ontario Parks using a ministry socio-economic impact model.

Although figures comparable to recreation/tourism are not currently available for the forest industry for 1996/97, it is known that the total impact of this activity in 1991/92 (East Side Wilderness Study) was in the order of $70.0 million (In this same period the impact for the public part of the recreation/tourism industry was in the order of $50.0 million). The employment opportunities created by the forest industry occurred primarily within the communities immediately adjacent to the park.

Since the socio-economic impact of these two Park-based industries is substantial both regionally and provincially it is important to continue to maintain and upgrade these industries to enhance their contribution. It is also important to ensure that the Park has an up to date analysis of the total socio-economic impact of these industries. Therefore, studies will be undertaken to determine these impacts prior to the next management plan review.

11.3 Plan Implementation

From a recreation/tourism perspective the implementation of this Park Management Plan is crucial to maintaining the socio-economic impact of the Park. The following Ancillary Plans will be developed, revised and/or completed to assist overall park management plan implementation: Aggregrate Resources, Water, Vegetation, Wildlife, Fisheries, Cultural Resources, Forest Management and Research.

In addition, a comprehensive ecosystem management strategy is being developed to ensure that park zoning, natural and cultural heritage protection, and recreational and forest management are dealt with in an integrated fashion.

Projects and activities that may be proposed for the Park but lack specific direction in the Park Management Plan or Ancillary Plans will be examined for their conformance with provincial park system policies, the objectives of the Park Management Plan and other relevant Ministry policies. Their potential environmental impacts will be assessed in terms of effects on the Park and the surrounding area.

In the implementation of this plan, the *Environmental Assessment Act*, Environmental Bill of Rights and other legal requirements will be adhered to at all times. The Algonquin Provincial Park Management Plan will be reviewed at least once every 10 years, but more frequent reviews may occur if deemed necessary. Minor amendments to the plan may be made at any time, should the need be identified, following the prescribed planning process. Major amendments will be subject to public consultation.

Nevertheless, the actual implementation of the projects and activities described in this Plan and any ancillary plans is dependent on the availability and allocation of funding in accordance with priorities established by Algonquin Park, the Ministry of Natural Resources and the Government of Ontario.

12.0 Public Consultation

The planning process for Algonquin Park has included many internal reviews and several public reviews. Internal reviews by Park staff have generated small operational/administrative changes or proposed larger development or management issues for public review. Public reviews provide a means for Park managers to determine the public's opinion on specific issues, and current and future management and development policies.

12.1 Algonquin Park Master Plan – 1974

Initially, Algonquin Park operated under a series of internal Department of Lands and Forests management and development plans. In 1966, work was begun on an official master plan for the Park. A provisional Master Plan was released on November 4, 1968 for public review, and public hearings were held in Pembroke, Huntsville and Toronto. The **Algonquin Park Task Force (APATAF)** was subsequently appointed to prepare a revised provisional Master Plan for the period January 1, 1970 to December 31, 1974 and to undertake background studies that would lead to the production of a final Master Plan by January 1, 1975. The task force also provided recommendations for immediate operating decisions and a report entitled *Interim Guidelines for Planning and Management* in December 1970.

In August 1969, the **Algonquin Park Advisory Committee**, a government-appointed body with representatives from a wide variety of interest groups, was established. This Committee was given a mandate to undertake studies and advise the Department of Lands and Forests on management policies for the Park. APATAF assisted the Committee by providing the background studies and information. By July 1973, the Committee had completed its work and submitted a report, entitled the *Algonquin Provincial Park Advisory Committee Report: Government Policy*, which contained 36 specific recommendations concerning the management of the Park. These recommendations and APATAF's information studies provided the direction and background for completion of the 1974 Algonquin Park Master Plan.

The completed **1974 Algonquin Park Master Plan** established detailed policy guidelines for the protection, management and future development of the Park. However, to ensure that the plan remained current and relevant, periodic reviews were carried out.

12.2 Master Plan Review – 1979

In 1979, the first public review of the Master Plan was carried out by the **Provincial Parks Council**, a citizens' advisory body. The Council reviewed letters from the public and chaired seven public meetings at which 1,123 people attended and 167 formal briefs were presented. After evaluating the public input in conjunction with other relevant background information, the Council presented 102 recommendations dealing with 35 different issues to the Minister of Natural Resources for his consideration. These recommendations and the Minister's response are outlined in the *Parks Council's Fifth Annual Report*.

Results of the review included: close the Lake of Two Rivers Airfield; continue to allow mechanical devices for portage aids; upgrade and expand the interpretive museum and logging exhibit; eliminate the Madawaska Motor Trail and upgrade Highway 60; administer campsites at the Kiosk, Achray and Brent perimeter access points as car campgrounds; continue to allow the use of hydro line right-of-way for snowmobile use; provide full-time administration of remote access points; empower Interior rangers to enforce all regulations; allow no new concession facilities; retain Clyde and Bruton Townships in the Park; and allow hunting to continue until a policy on hunting in all provincial parks was drafted. During this review, the application of the 1978 *Ontario Provincial Parks Planning and Management Policies* to Algonquin Park was also described.

12.3 Review of Cottage Leaseholds – 1986

In 1986, the Provincial Parks Council reviewed the terms of the **Cottage Leasehold Policies** for Algonquin and Rondeau Provincial Parks and recommended that the long-term goal of phasing out cottages in Algonquin Park be maintained. The Minister agreed with this recommendation to terminate the leases in or before the year 2017. Conditions attached to the renewal of the leases also included: rents would be based on fair market values; leases would be subject to the standards of maintenance and construction as deemed appropriate by the Park Superintendent; and written approval would be required for any lease transfers, improvements, landscaping, excavations or earth moving.

12.4 Pre-1989 Review Amendments

In 1983 the Master Plan was first amended to more adequately protect the Swan Lake Forest Research Area by including it within the Parkway Development Zone rather than the Recreation/Utilization Zone. In 1988 the Plan was amended to permit the development of the new Visitor Centre and Logging Museum (in place of the historic Mowat Complex proposed in the 1974 plan). In 1989, in response to the recommendations of the 1979 Review, the existing Wilderness Zone boundary was modified to *exclude* two existing non-conforming uses — Arowhon Pines Lodge and Sasajewun Wildlife Research Station. The boundary of the Parkway Development Zone was extended to enclose these two facilities, slightly reducing the size of the Wilderness Zone. Also in 1989 an amendment was approved to permit the development of three new interpretive trails along Highway 60 (supported by the 1979 Review).

12.5 Master Plan Review – 1989

In May 1989, the Minister of Natural Resources once again asked the **Provincial Parks Council** to undertake a public review of the Algonquin Park Master Plan. Eight public meetings were held with a total of 802 people in attendance, and 87 briefs were presented by individuals, groups or organizations. The Council also received numerous letters from interested parties and 1,904 questionnaire responses from the 54,000 tabloids distributed to Ministry offices, Park visitors and 482 interest groups and individuals on the Park's mailing list. After an analysis of the public input and relevant information, the Council made 117 recommendations dealing with 37 issues to the Minister.

Results of the review included: phase out public hunting, hunt camps and trapping in Clyde and Bruton Townships and the McRae Addition by 2010; impose 20 horsepower limits on all but two unlimited horsepower lakes; ban water skiing; revise the Interior quota system; upgrade existing facilities in the Park; establish Areas of Concern around the Park; introduce other recreational activities to the Park, such as mountain bike trails and horseback riding trails; study the development needs of the peripheral areas of the Park; promote new marketing initiatives through facilities such as a new Park lodge, skill development centre or alternative accommodations; add approximately 10,000 hectares to Nature Reserve Zones; and conduct a Wilderness Zone study on the east side of the Park.

12.6 Post-1989 Review Amendments

In response to the 1989 Review, action was taken to implement a number of the key recommendations through amendments to the 1974 Master Plan.

A review of the earth and life science value/feature representation in the Park's system of Nature Reserve Zones resulted in a net increase in the total area of the Nature Reserve Zones. Following on the recommendations of D. F. Brunton, a life science consultant, several new zones were added and existing ones enlarged to provide greater site district representation. The boundaries of a number of the zones were also modified to provide more ecologically reasonable boundaries (easily identifiable on the ground). Some zones were excluded from the new system because the studies established that the zone boundaries did not include the feature originally designated for protection (e.g., Weasel Lake White Pine) or because the feature was not substantiated (e.g., Carl Wilson Addition). Also, as a result of the recommendations of C. M. Spek, an earth science consultant, 14 Nature Reserve Zones and 26 Special Management Areas were established to protect earth science features and values. These Nature Reserve Zone changes were implemented through a plan amendment in 1992.

As a result of the Algonquin Park East Side Wilderness Zone Study, recommended in the 1989 Review, five candidate wilderness zones were identified on the east side of the Park. These candidates had the potential to provide additional protection of east-side natural and cultural values and to act as an area of wilderness where natural processes could continue uninterrupted in the presence of Interior recreation use. Of the five candidate areas, the Lavieille-Dickson candidate was far superior and was approved in 1993 and established as a new Wilderness Zone in 1994 through a plan amendment.

In 1994, a plan amendment was approved to develop a new bicycle trail along the bed of the old Ottawa, Arnprior & Parry Sound Railway between the Mew Lake and Rock Lake campgrounds in the Park.

The Petawawa River west of Lake Travers

12.7 Algonquin Park Management Plan

The new **Algonquin Park Management Plan** is a composite of the old Master Plan and changes proposed in the 1979 and 1989 reviews (changes introduced in the 1989 Review supersede changes made during the 1979 Review). This Plan incorporates all amendments made to date. The Plan has also been revised to conform with the standard Park Management Plan format and to incorporate changes in zoning policies as a result of the *Ontario Provincial Parks Planning and Management Policies* introduced in May 1978 and revised in 1992.

Some of the more notable differences in the Plan as a result of recommendations from previous reviews include an increase in the area of Nature Reserve Zones, the creation of a new Wilderness Zone, the introduction of Natural Environment Zones and the reduction/addition of some Development Zones.

Natural Environment Zones permit back-country activities while excluding high-intensity development and resource-extraction activities. This type of zone was established to replace areas in Development Zones that would not be developed in the future and to create buffers between Development Zones and other zones. A reduced Development Zone — the Achray Development Zone — and the new Stratton Lake Natural Environment Zone have replaced the former Stratton Lake Development Zone, an area that was determined to be unsuitable for campground development.

The Lake Travers Natural Environment Zones were established to create a buffer between the Lake Travers developments and adjacent Nature Reserve Zones. Several Natural Environment Zones were also established along the Parkway Corridor to replace areas of the Development Zone that will not be used for future development.

In addition to some of the reductions in the **Development Zones** mentioned earlier, some new Development Zones are established in this Plan. In the 1989 Master Plan Review, campgrounds at several access points were recommended to be retained at or above their present capacity and upgraded. Further development studies were also recommended for the peripheral areas of the Park to provide economic benefits to local communities. Therefore, in those areas of existing campground development and to accommodate future development, Development Zones were established in the Kiosk, Achray and Brent areas. Since Rain Lake is primarily used for Interior access and has few sites and limited capacity for expansion, it is retained as an Access Zone.

The Park Management Plan and the noted implementation plans will meet the applicable requirements of the *Environmental Assessment Act* and the Environmental Bill of Rights. Subsequent reviews of the Algonquin Park Management Plan will be undertaken every 10 years. However, changes may be made to the Plan as the need arises and in accordance with the policy requirements for public review.

The production of this Management Plan has been delayed by many factors. The province's financial situation, the restructuring of the Ministry and changes made with the creation of the Ontario Parks agency have all contributed to the delay. However, this Plan stands as a significant consolidation of Algonquin Park policy. This Plan will serve as the official working document for the day to day administration and management of the Park from the day that it is approved. Any concerns with the directions taken for the implementation of any new or amended policies can be brought to the attention of the Park Superintendent and will be dealt with through the next Park Management Plan Review.

APPENDIX A
Construction and Development Standards Algonquin Park Cottage Leaseholds

Purpose of Standards

These standards are intended to clarify specific information as to type, number and size of improvements that will be permitted on a lease and to outline requirements of the approval process.

When Approval Required

Algonquin Park leases contain conditions that require the approval of the Park Superintendent prior to carrying out such activities as building, additions or improvement to existing buildings, docks, shoreline work and cutting of vegetation and landscaping.

Approval Process

Such approval will be in the form of a work permit. Applications for a work permit are available from the staff at the East Gate. An application must be accompanied by properly prepared plans of the work and must be submitted at least 30 days prior to the anticipated start-up date to enable an adequate review. Plans will include: the location of all existing buildings, size, setback from water and type of construction. **Applications improperly completed will be returned.**

Standards

These standards were developed after a review of zoning by-laws and construction standards in municipalities adjoining the Park and are provided for reference when considering improvements and for guidance in the preparation of an application.

1. Only one "cottaging unit" (1) will be allowed per leased lot (existing situations will remain, but any upgrading/ redevelopment will be judged on a case by case basis).
2. A new or replacement "self-contained cottage" (2) shall not exceed 119 square metres (1280 square feet).
3. A new or replacement "sleep cabin" (3) shall not exceed 22.3 square metres (240 square feet).
4. Applications for replacement sleep cabins on leases that currently have more than one cottaging unit will be judged on a case by case basis.
5. All new or replacement self-contained cottages and sleep cabins must be located a minimum of 20 metres (66 feet) from the water's edge. Requests for replacements will be judged on a case by case basis.
6. Applications for new boathouses on the water will not be approved. Requests for replacements will be judged on a case by case basis pending a site review.
7. New boathouses shall not contain sleeping quarters, kitchen or toilet facilities.
8. The height of all buildings shall not exceed one storey, with an inside bearing wall not exceeding 2.44 metres (8 feet).
9. New buildings shall be painted, stained and shingled in a colour that will blend with the natural surroundings (e.g., dark brown or green). Existing buildings of non-compatible colour will be brought into conformity with these standards at the time of repainting.
10. The installation of sewage disposal facilities will be considered. All installations must be approved and installed in accordance with the standards of the Ministry of Environment and requests for installation must be accompanied by MOE approval.
11. All waste water from sinks, showers, etc. (gray water) must not be discharged directly into the lake and must be disposed of in properly constructed dry wells.
12. Requests for tent platforms will be judged on a case by case basis.

General

- ⇨ The aesthetic impact of any proposal will form part of the review process.
- ⇨ The planting of non-indigenous tree species is not permitted.
- ⇨ Projects that would involve disruption of fish habitat will not be approved (docks).

Ontario must comply with the *Federal Fisheries Act*. This Act ensures Canadian fisheries are protected by maintaining a "no net loss of habitat" policy. Fishery habitat is defined as "spawning grounds and nursery, rearing, food supply and migration areas on which fish depend directly or indirectly in order to carry out their life processes." It has therefore become increasingly more critical to review requests for work in and along water in a different way in order to prevent harmful alteration or destruction of fish habitat. In areas where habitat precludes a construction project, cantilever or floating docks may be an acceptable alteration.

Definitions

(1) "Cottaging Unit" — consists of one main cottage, a sleep cabin, a boathouse and one shed.
(2) "Self-Contained Cottage" — a building designed for use by one family and may have one or more habitable rooms, including a kitchen, sanitary facilities and common sitting area for exclusive use of the family. Such a building may be used for vacation, recreation, rest and relaxation but shall not be used as a year-round dwelling.
(3) "Sleep Cabin" — a habitable building or structure designed to provide accommodation and that is an accessory to a permitted main cottage. It shall contain no form of cooking, kitchen facilities or washroom facilities and no common sitting area.

APPENDIX B
Construction and Development Standards Algonquin Park Commercial Leaseholds

Purpose of Standards

These standards are intended to clarify specific information as to type, number and size of improvements that will be permitted on a lease and to outline requirements of the approval process.

When Approval Required

Algonquin Park leases contain conditions that require approval of the Park Superintendent prior to carrying out such activities as building, additions or improvement to existing buildings, docks, shoreline work and cutting of vegetation and landscaping.

Approval Process

Such approval will be in the form of a work permit. Applications for a work permit are available from the staff at the East Gate. An application must be accompanied by properly prepared plans of the work and must be submitted at least 30 days prior to the anticipated start-up date to enable an adequate review. Plans will include: the location of all existing buildings, size, setback from water and type of construction. **Applications improperly completed will be returned.**

Standards

These standards were developed after a review of zoning by-laws and construction standards in municipalities adjoining the Park and are provided for reference when considering improvements and for guidance in the preparation of an application.

1. All new or replacement self-contained cottages and sleep cabins must be located a minimum of 20 metres (66 feet) from the water's edge. Requests for replacements will be judged on a case by case basis.
2. Applications for new boathouses **on the water** will not be approved. Requests for replacments will be judged on a case by case basis pending a site review.
3. New boathouses shall not contain sleeping quarters, kitchen or toilet facilities.
4. The height of all buildings shall not exceed one storey, with an inside bearing wall not exceeding 2.44 metres (8 feet).
5. New buildings shall be painted, stained and shingled in a colour that will blend with the natural surroundings (e.g., dark brown or green). Existing buildings of non-compatible colour will be brought into conformity with these standards at the time of repainting.
6. The installation of sewage disposal facilities will be considered. All installations must be approved and installed in accordance with standards of the Ministry of Environment and requests for installation must be accompanied by MOE approval.
7. All waste water from sinks, showers, etc. (gray water) must not be discharged directly into the lake and must be disposed of in properly constructed dry wells.
8. Requests for tent platforms will be judged on a case by case basis.

General

- ⇨ The aesthetic impact of any proposal will form part of the review process.
- ⇨ The planting of non-indigenous tree species is not permitted.
- ⇨ Projects that would involve disruption of fish habitat will not be approved (docks).

Ontario must comply with the *Federal Fisheries Act*. This Act ensures Canadian fisheries are protected by maintaining a "no net loss of habitat" policy. Fishery habitat is defined as "spawning grounds and nursery, rearing, food supply and migration areas on which fish depend directly or indirectly in order to carry out their life processes." It has therefore become increasingly more critical to review requests for work in and along water in a different way in order to prevent harmful alteration or destruction of fish habitat. In areas where habitat precludes a construction project, cantilever or floating docks may be an acceptable alteration.

APPENDIX C
Guidelines for Resource Management and Land Use Activities along the Perimeter of Algonquin Park (see also Section 5.0)

Guideline Principles:

1) The goals and objectives of Algonquin Provincial Park will provide the basis for ensuring the protection of values within the Park.

2) Land use activities will not be unduly restricted, but rather resource management activities will be encouraged to take place in a manner that does not have a negative impact on Park values.

Park Goal and Objectives:

The Goal of Algonquin Provincial Park is:

To provide protection of natural and cultural features, continuing opportunities for a diversity of low-intensity recreational, wilderness, and natural environmental experiences and, within this provision, continue and enhance the Park's contribution to the economic, social and cultural life of the region.

The Objectives of Algonquin Provincial Park are:

Protection Objective:

To protect provincially significant elements of the natural and cultural landscape of Algonquin Park.

Recreation Objective:

To provide outdoor recreation opportunities ranging from high-intensity day use to low-intensity wilderness experiences.

Heritage Appreciation Objective:

To provide opportunities for exploration and appreciation of the outdoor natural and cultural heritage of Algonquin Park.

Tourism Objective:

To provide Ontario's residents and out-of-province visitors with opportunities to discover and experience the distinctive regions of Algonquin Park.

Resource Management Objective:

To practise sustainable resource management in Algonquin Park for the long-term health of the Park's ecosystems and to provide recreational, cultural and economic benefits.

Protection of Values Within the Park:

Protection of values within the Park can be addressed through the Management Plan, public reviews, Park policy and existing legislation and guidelines. Examples of existing legislation and guidelines include: *Provincial Parks Act, Environmental Protection Act, Ontario Water Resources Act, Lake and Rivers Improvement Act, Fisheries Act, Mining Amendment Act*, as well as the *Environmental Guidelines for Access Roads and Water Crossings, Timber Management Guidelines for the Protection of Fish Habitat, Timber Management Guidelines for the Protection of Tourism Values, Timber Management Guidelines for the Protection of Cultural Heritage Resources* and *Timber Management Guidelines for the Provision of Moose Habitat.* Other Acts and regulations that may also have applicability include the *Municipal Act, Planning Act, Public Health Act* and *Highway Traffic Act.*

Legislation and guidelines can also be used to regulate activities outside the Park to ensure that Park values are protected. Districts bordering Algonquin Park will consult with the Algonquin Park Office on any development or management activities proposed near the Park that may affect its values. Values within the Park that can be affected by adjacent land use and that are important to the achievement of the goal and objectives of Algonquin Provincial Park include:

1) Environmental Values:

Water Quality, Water Levels

Activities or development occurring on or adjacent to waterbodies entering Algonquin Park (e.g., Tim River) have the greatest potential to affect the Park's natural water quality. Input into water quality and water level concerns will be through existing legislation and guidelines. However, additional setbacks or provisions may be requested.

2) Aesthetic Values:

Visual, Acoustic

The aesthetic values of Algonquin Park contribute directly to the recreational values of the Park and thus the recreational opportunities for Park visitors. Visitors perceive a natural or semi-wilderness setting. These aesthetic values may be affected by changes in water quality and unnatural visual conditions or noises. Land use activities immediately adjacent to the Park have the greatest potential to affect aesthetic values. Potential impacts will be reviewed and mitigated by such means as adjusting operating practices or altering the timing of the activity.

3) Social Values:
Crowding, Travel Patterns, User Activities, User Characteristics

New and unplanned access to the Park has the potential to seriously and negatively impact the Park's social values. This includes direct access (immediately adjacent to the Park) or indirect access (through an outside water source). Unplanned access to Algonquin Provincial Park will be avoided by input to and review of plans for road locations and standards. Access restrictions, such as the posting of signs or the use of a gate, are not acceptable if the road in question would lead to a watercourse or waterbody ultimately leading into the Park. There should be no access impact problems for the Park if a road were proposed for an area that was not near a watercourse or waterbody.

Assessment of Activities or Developments along the perimeter of Algonquin Park

Description of Proposed Activity:

Location:

Assessment:

1) Are there any concerns about water quality or water levels that have not already been dealt with by existing legislation or guidelines?
2) Are there potential acoustic or visual impacts to be mitigated?
3) Is there potential for unplanned access to the Park that needs to be mitigated?

Recommendation

Yes ______ No ______

Recommended Mitigation Plan:

Assessed by: ____________________________

Date: ________________

Mitigation Plan Approved by: ____________________________

Date: ________________

APPENDIX D
Significant Earth and Life Science Sites in Algonquin Park

ZONE		AREA (HA)	NATURAL VALUES AND FEATURES Community/Complex/Landform	
			Life Science	Earth Science
1. NATURE RESERVE ZONES				
N-1	Cameron Creek Bog	165	Wetland complex-P	
N-2	David Creek Bog	214	Peatland complex-P	
N-3	Sunkitten Lake Bog	240	Peatland complex-L	
N-4	Keegos Lake Bog	418	Peatland complex-P	
N-5	Thomas Lake Kettle Bog	17	Peatland-L	
N-6	Hogan Lake Mog	770	Wetland complex-P	Morainic Ridges-L
N-7	Bonanza Bay Marsh	92	Marsh & deciduous swamp forest-P	
N-8	Grand Lake Marsh	51	Wetland complex-R	
N-9	Cedar-Nipissing Marsh	121	Marsh complex-P	
N-10	Costello Creek Bog	614	Wetland & granitic Outcrop complex-R	
N-11	Grassy Bay Mog	942	Wetland-L	Kame complex-L
N-12	Hailstorm Creek & Kame Complex	1613	Wetland complex-P	Kame complex-R
N-13	Booth Lake Bog	319	Wetland complex-R	
N-14	Bonnechere Sedge Meadow	31	Wetland complex-R	
N-15	Clyde Marsh	183	Wetland & cliff complex-R	
N-16	Carcajou Sedge Meadow	133	Wetland complex-R	
N-17	Nipissing River Sedge Meadow	180	Wetland complex-R	
N-18	Kingscote Lake Hardwoods	96	Hardwood forest-R	
N-19	Nadine Lake Hardwoods	1091	Upland hardwood & Shoreline complex-P	
N-20	Carl Wilson L. Hardwoods	504	Upland forest & outcrop complex-P	
N-21	Dickson Lake Hardwoods	104	Upland forest & wetland complex-P	
N-22	Minto Lake Hardwoods	259	Upland forest-R	
N-23	Wenda Lake Hardwoods	730	Upland forest-P	
N-24	Whitson Lake	755	Upland, lowland forest & wetland complex-P	
N-25	Oxtongue River Silver Maple	144	Lowland forest-L	
N-26	Rana Lake Red Oak	487	Upland forest-P	
N-27	McManus Lake Basswood	47	Upland forest & shore vegetation-R	
N-28	Wilkes Lake Basswood	28	Upland forest-L	
N-29	Hurdman Creek Black Ash	63	Lowland forest complex-R	
N-30	Dickson Lake	39	Upland forest-P	
N-31	Cayuga Lake Hemlock	660	Upland forest complex-P	
N-32	Dividing Lake/Livingstone Township White Pine	496(*)	Upland forest & old growth-P	
N-33	Big Crow White Pine	208	Upland forest-P	
N-34	Old Pine Reserve	78	Upland forest-R	

(*) Majority of this area is protected outside Algonquin Park through Dividing Lake Provincial Park

**Significance: N = national, P = provincial, R = regional, L = local

ZONE	AREA (HA)	NATURAL VALUES AND FEATURES Community/Complex/Landform Life Science	Earth Science
N-35 Anglin-Dickson White Pine	290	Upland forest-P	
N-36 Carl Wilson White Pine & Kame Moraine	256	Upland forest Complex-R	Kame moraine-R
N-37 Crow River Young Wh. Pine	38	Upland forest-L	
N-38 Nipissing Valley Wh. Pine	24	Upland forest-L	
N-40 Lavieillé Red Pine	79	Upland forest-R	
N-41 Opeongo Red Pine	104	Upland forest Upland forest-L	
N-42 Crow River Jack Pine	33	Upland forest-L	
N-43 Bonnechere Jack Pine	47	Upland forest-R	
N-44 Carcajou Jack Pine	398	Upland forest-P	
N-45 Cauliflower Lake Red Spruce	25	Upland & lowland Forest complex-L	
N-46 Bruton and Clyde Red Spruce	585	Upland forest complex-P	
N-47 Oak Lake Red Spruce	174	Upland forest & Wetland complex-P	
N-48 Rosebary Lake	746	Beach & upland Forest complex-P	
N-49 Tarn Lake	1483	Upland forest, open outcrop & wetland complex-P	
N-50 Carcajou Bay/ Spectacle Lakes	1084	Upland forest & wetland complex-P	
N-51 Devils Chute	542	Upland & shoreline complex-R	
N-52 Found Lake	95	Floristic site-R	
N-53 Upper Pine River	1109	Wetland & intolerant upland forest complex-P	
N-54 High Falls	100	Upland complex-L	
N-55 Petawawa Rapids	1927	Upland forest, lowland & shoreline complex-P	Part of Ottawa Bonnechere Graben (fault)-R
N-56 Bog Lemming Site	18	Mammal population-L	
N-57 Barron River Canyon	1076	Upland forest and outcrop complex-P	Part of Ottawa Bonnechere Graben (fault)-R, talus-L
N-58 White Partridge Cliff	100	Floristic site-R	
N-59 Crow Lake Cliff	40	Cliff complex-R	
N-60 Eustache Lake	835	Aquatic & upland complex-P	
N-61 Hilliard Lake Fern Stand	33	Floristic site-R	
N-62 Brent Crater	1199	Upland and lowland complex-P	Meteor crater-L
N-63 Brent Limestone Cliff	8	Bedrock complex-R	
N-64 Tim River Burn	1014	Upland meadow complex-P	
N-65 Cauchon Lake Burn	263	Upland & forest complex-R	

**Significance: N = national, P = provincial, R = regional, L = local

ZONE	AREA (HA)	NATURAL VALUES AND FEATURES Community/Complex/Landform Life Science	Earth Science
N-66 Merchant Lake Blowdown	96	Upland forest-L	
N-67 Crow Lake Blowdown	609	Natural succession process-R(SD 5E-9) - L(SD 5E-10)	
N-68 Manitou Lake Blowdown	112	Upland forest-L	
N-69 Coldspring Watershed	4914	Watershed unit-P	Kame moraine & eskers-R
N-70 Greenleaf Crk Watershed	4041	Watershed-P	Moraine-L
N-71 Berm Lake Bog	53	Peatland-R	
N-72 Charles Lake White Pine	102	Forest stand-R	
N-73 Lake Lavieillé Hemlock	45	Upland forest-P	
N-74 Lake Travers Dune Complex	59	Upland forest & Wetland-P	Inland dune field -P (see N-85)
N-75 Mud Bay Aquatics	131	Aquatic floristic complex-R	
N-76 Spoor Lake	552	Upland & wetland complex-P	
N-77 Chainfern Bog	17	Wetland-R	
N-78 Minnehaha Lake Kame Moraine	839		Glaciofluvial landforms (eskers, kettles, kame moraines)-R
N-80 Loontail Lake Gravelly Moraine	490		Gravelly moraine-R
N-81 Wilkes L. Ice Marginal Delta	99		Kame complex-R
N-82 Robitaille Creek Terraces	95		Erosional terraces-R
N-84 Lake Travers DeGeer Moraines	178		Degeer-type moraines-P
N-85 Lake Travers Sand Dunes	314		Inland dune field-P
N-86 Radiant L. Kame Terrace	176		Ice contact kame Terraces-P
N-87 Big Crow L. Esker Complex	260		Esker complex-R
N-88 White Partridge Lake Erosional Terraces	245		Erosional terraces-P
N-89 McKaskill L. Kame Complex	259		Kame-esker complex, Ice contact face-R
N-90 Grand Lake Ice Marginal Channels	183		Ice marginal channels-R
N-91 Fitzgerald Township Moraine	226		Large moraine-R

Although the above list of nature reserve zones is numbered consecutively, there are three zones missing — 39, 79 and 83. These zones have been either combined with other zones or been deleted from the list because further studies have shown that the values to be protected no longer exist within the area of the zone.

**Significance: N = national, P = provincial, R = regional, L = local

ZONE	AREA (HA)	NATURAL VALUES AND FEATURES Community/Complex/Landform Life Science	 Earth Science
2. SPECIAL MANAGEMENT AREAS (SMA)			
CLASS I			
Petawawa Terraces	318		Erosional terraces-R
Sunfish L. Morainic Ridge	91		Small moraine-L
Grosbeak Creek Outwash/Kame T.	546		Ice contact material, eskers, kettle-R
North Rouge Creek Drumlins	1697		Drumlins, drumlinoidal features-R
Grassy Bay Kame Complex	(737*)		Kame-esker complex-L
Radiant Lake Kame Terraces	508		Kame esker complex-R
Proulx Lake Outwash	492		Outwash plain, kame complex-R
Modern Fluvial Deltas (3)	69		Modern fluvial deposits-L
Grand Lake Boulder Pavement	42		Boulder lag-R
Achray Beaches/Deposits	37		Beach ridges, off-shore deposits-L
Lake Travers Outwash Plain	7416		Glaciofluvial landforms-R
White Partridge L. Spillway	3185		Outwash plain, meltwater channels-L
Notsolong Lake Esker	299		Large esker-L
Hogan Lake Esker	225		Esker kame-L

(*) Protected within N-11 Nature Reserve and Burnt Island Wilderness Zones

ZONE	AREA (HA)	Life Science	Earth Science
CLASS II			
Coldspring L/Carl Wilson Complex	11640		Kame-esker complex-R
Biggar Twp Gravelly Moraine	13414		Gravelly moraine-R
Clemow Lake Drumlin Group	91		Drumlins-R
Indian River Meltwater Channel	2730		Meltwater channel-R
Bonnechere Valley Outwash System	2933		Outwash system-R
Booth Lake Delta	128		Outwash delta-R
Lake of Two Rivers Outwash Plain	1391		Outwash plain-L
Oxtongue River Outwash Plain	(674*)		Outwash plain-L
Brent Fluted Till Plain	150		Fluted till, drumlins-R
Bronson-Stratton Outwash Plain	7575		Outwash plain, meltwater channels-R
Forbes Creek Meltwater Channel	1911		Meltwater channel-L
Grand Lake Tombolo	22		Tombolo-L

(*) Protected within the Parkway Development Zone

ZONE	AREA (HA)	Life Science	Earth Science
3. WILDERNESS ZONES			
Galeairy Wilderness Zone	5280		Landscape complex-P
Harness Lake Wilderness Zone	10960		Landscape complex-P
Burnt Island Wilderness Zone	48870		Upland forest-R kame complexes-R,L
Laviellé/Dickson Wilderness Zone	25365		Landscape complex & old growth pine-P

**Significance: N = national, P = provincial, R = regional, L = local

APPENDIX E
Historical Zones in Algonquin Park

Zone Number	Description of Value	Location	Township
H-1	Fassett Lake Lumber Camp	S. of Fassett Lake	Ballantyne
H-2	Amable du Fond Farm	N. of Manitou Lake	Wilkes
H-3	Pentland Skidway	S. of Lauder Lake	Pentland
H-4	Meda Lake Lumber Camp	E. of Meda Lake	Biggar
H-5	Brent Grave Site	Brent	Lister
H-6	Pine River Farm	Tim River	Devine
H-7	McLachlin Depot Farm	N. of Trout River	Bishop
H-8	Barnet Depot Farm	S. of Burntrout Lake	Bishop
H-9	Phillip's Depot Farm	E. of Phillip Lake	Anglin
H-10	Phillip's Chute	E. of Phillip Lake	Anglin
H-11	Turtle Club	S. of Lake Travers	White
H-12	Crooked Chute	Petawawa River	Edgar
H-13	Captain Young's Depot Farm	W. of Emma Lake	Edgar
H-14	Mackey Farm	W. of Trout Lake	McLaughlin
H-15	Crossbill Lake Lumber	Crossbill Lake	McLaughlin
H-16	Graham Creek Chute	Graham Creek (W. of Opeongo)	Bower
H-17	Dennison Farm	E. arm Opeongo Lake	Bower
H-18	Little Dickson L. Camboose Camp	Little Dickson Lake	Dickson
H-19	Prong Lake Bridge	N. of Prong Lake	Niven
H-20	Bonnechere R. Camboose Camp	Bonnechere River	Niven
H-21	McLachlin Depot Farm	N. of Grand Lake	Barron
H-22	Grand Lake Indian Pictographs	E. of Grand Lake	Stratton
H-23	Tom Thomson Jack Pine Site	Grand Lake	Stratton
H-24	Grand Lake Ranger Cabin	Achray	Stratton
H-25	Whiskey Rapids	Oxtongue River	Peck
H-26	Mowat Town Site	N. of Canoe Lake	Peck
H-27	Nominigan Lodge Site	Smoke Lake	Peck
H-28	Ottawa, Arnprior & P.S. Railway	S. of Hwy. 60	Canisbay
H-29	Canisbay Lake Cabin	Logging Museum	Airy
H-30	McCrae's Mill	S. of Hwy. 60	Canisbay
H-31	W. Smith Lake Sawmill	West Smith Lake	Sproule
H-32	Annie Bay Camboose Camp	S. of Annie Bay	Preston
H-33	Annie Bay Shanty & Farm	Annie Bay on Opeongo	Preston
H-34	Tattler-Booth Crib	W. of Booth Lake	Preston
H-35	Presto Lake Lumber Camp	Presto Lake	Preston
H-36	Kitty Lake Ranger Cabin	S. of Kitty Lake	Preston
H-37	Booth Depot Farm	W. of Farm Lake	Preston
H-38	McCauley Central Railway	W. of Farm Lake	Preston
H-39	Billy Lake Lumber	N. of Billy Lake	Preston
H-40	Ryan Lake Lumber Camp	Ryan Lake	Preston
H-41	McKaskill Lake Ranger Cabin	S. of McKaskill Lake	Clancy
H-42	Basin Depot Farm	S. of Basin Lake	Guthrie
H-43	Upper Pine Lake Ranger Cabin	Upper Pine Lake	Master
H-44	Rock Lake Cairns	W. of Rock Lake	Nightingale
H-45	Rock Lake Indian Pictographs	W. of Rock Lake	Nightingale
H-46	Rock Lake Indian Pictographs	W. of Rock Lake	Nightingale
H-47	Farm Bay Depot	S. of Galeairy Lake	Nightingale
H-48	Pioneer Logging Exhibit	H. Hwy. 69 near East Gate	Airy

APPENDIX F

Forest Management Strategies for Each Park Zone

Park Zone	Zone Definition	Forest Management		Forest Management Strategies
		Yes	No	
Nature Reserve	Nature Reserve Zones include any significant earth and/or life science features that require management different from that in adjacent zones.		X	■ no road building permitted
Wilderness	Wilderness Zones include wilderness landscapes of appropriate size and integrity that protect significant natural and cultural features and are suitable for wilderness experiences.		X	■ no road building permitted
Natural Environment	Natural Environment Zones include aesthetic, natural and cultural landscapes in which there is minimum development required to support low-intensity backcountry recreational activities.		X	■ no road building permitted
Historical	Historical Zones include any significant historical resources that require management distinct from that in adjacent zones.		X	■ no road building permitted
Development	Development Zones provide the main access to the Park and the facilities and services for a wide range of day-use and camping activities.		X	■ no new forest access roads permitted
Access	Access Zones serve as staging areas where minimum facilities support use of nature reserve and wilderness zones, less-developed natural environment, historical and recreation/utilization zones.		X	■ no new forest access roads permitted
Recreation/ Utilization	Recreation-Utilization Zones include aesthetic landscapes in which there is minimum development required to support low-intensity recreational activities while also providing for commercial timber harvesting.	X		■ special harvesting and road regulations have been developed to protect Park values and recreational activities and experiences. These regulations are listed in the following table.

Forest Management Strategies for Recreation/Utilization Zone

Forest Operations	■ between the last Saturday in June and Labour Day, both dates inclusive, road construction and cutting are prohibited within 1.6 kilometres of canoe routes and recreation trails. ■ during the same period, travel of loaded or unloaded haul trucks from and through the areas is restricted between 7:30 a.m. and 6:30 p.m. daylight saving time, Monday to Friday inclusive, statutory holidays exclusive. There are no hauling restrictions on, and north of, the Sand Lake Road between the Sand Lake Gate and the Petawawa River bridge at Lake Travers, as well as on all roads north of the Petawawa River and the chain of lakes connecting Lake Travers to Kioshkokwi Lake. ■ in harvest areas adjacent to high off-season recreational use areas or where the topography permits sound travel, noise restrictions may be adjusted in both the timing and distance of operations as determined at the Annual Work Schedule (AWS) stage. ■ the rafting of logs across lakes and the driving of rivers are prohibited in the Park.
Transportation of Forest Products	■ transportation of unmanufactured forest products from areas outside the Park to manufacturing facilities outside, via Algonquin roads, is permitted only over public roads in the Park.
Road Construction	■ roads will be developed in accordance with the permanent road system strategy. Tertiary roads will be pre-approved at the AWS stage. ■ no roads may be constructed within 120 metres (394 feet) of waters, portages, public roads, railway rights-of-way, and the Park boundary, except in accordance with the strategy for roads that cross canoe routes in the Interior. ■ roads or clearings will not be constructed within any Nature Reserve Zone, Wilderness Zone, or Historical Zone. Any existing roads will be phased out where possible. ■ roads no longer needed that cross portages, trails, and navigable or publicly-used streams will be rehabilitated to natural vegetation. ■ all timber must be cut and salvaged from road rights-of-way. ■ road crossings of canoeable waters will be by bridge with a minimum approach fill and clearance to preclude the need for portaging. ■ maximum rights-of-way clearing widths are: Type of Road — Right-of-Way Width Primary Road — 13.7 metres (45 feet) Secondary & Tertiary Road — 9.1 metres (30 feet) Roads Crossing Timber Reserves — 6.7 metres (22 feet) ■ roads between 120 and 460 metres (394 and 1 509 feet) of canoe routes have rights-of-way widths of 9.1 metres (30 feet). ■ existing roads (can be travelled by a conventional half-ton truck) will be used to access previously cut areas. ■ existing roads in the Recreation-Utilization Zone may be phased out if alternative means of access are available that have a lesser impact on Park values. ■ existing (as defined above) road crossings of the Park boundary, other than public access roads, may be phased out and no new road crossings will be permitted.

Forest Management Strategies for Recreation/Utilization Zone (cont'd)

Strategy for Roads Crossing Canoe Routes	■ the four classes of crossing of portages and constructions in navigable waterways are: i) no crossings ii) temporary winter crossing: ■ road built to harvest forest products and to conduct silvicultural operations at the time of cutting only. Road access for later tending operations is not considered. Crossing rehabilitation must be completed prior to the Victoria holiday weekend in May and carried out between Park operating seasons. Work on the crossing should not start before October 15. iii) temporary crossing: ■ road built to harvest forest products over an entire block using one silvicultural system or at intervals by another system. Road access for silvicultural operations at other than the time(s) of harvest should not be considered. Crossing rehabilitation and crossing development work as per the temporary winter crossing class dates and at the end of the harvest cut and between periodic harvest cuts. iv) permanent crossing: ■ no new crossings of portages or canoe routes will be allowed unless no other options are available and the trading of one crossing for another is not allowed. ■ an existing crossing may be eliminated if its existence is no longer justified.
Gravel Pits	■ maximum pit size of 1 hectare (2.5 acres). ■ In the construction of roads, fill may be taken within the road right-of-way and not below the water table. Borrow pits outside the road right-of-way may be permitted. To prevent excessive disturbance outside the road right-of-way, borrow pits will be limited to a maximum of five per kilometre. The size of borrow pits must not exceed 6 metres (19.7 feet) including side slopes of 1.5:1 and are limited to 10 metres (32.8 feet) from the tree-line of the road right-of-way. There will be no excavation below the ditch line of the road, and all slopes will be angles to the road wherever possible. If additional fill is required for road building, material will be supplied by approved aggregate pits. ■ aggregate material may not be used outside the Park. ■ pits are not permitted within 120 metres (394 feet) of a body of water and associated wetland complex, public road, railway right-of-way, portage, or hiking trail or within 60 metres (197 feet) of an MNR-maintained ski trail unless approved in an Aggregate Resource Management Plan. Prior to the completion of an Aggregate Resource Management Plan, aggregate pits within 120 metres of a body of water or wetland may also be approved contingent upon the review of earth and life science studies of the area, as well as hydrological and other environmental impact studies of the site.
Landings	■ landings for logs shall not exceed 0.2 of a hectare (0.5 of an acre) in size.

Forest Management Strategies for Recreation/Utilization Zone (cont'd)

Concentration Yards	▪ Sawmills, concentration yards, and secondary manufacturing facilities are prohibited in the Park. Existing concentration yards, which include Daventry and Peck, will be phased out by 1995, and L. Travers and Odenback will be phased out once they are no longer required or alternative locations outside the Park are established. The AFA will ensure that: existing concentration yards will not exceed 5 hectares (12.4 acres); will not be used after the long weekend in July and before Labour Day; all debris will be disposed of as fuelwood, burned, chipped, mulched, or removed on a continuous basis; and site rehabilitation will be completed once the site has been abandoned. Portable chipping will be permitted but will be subject to sound zone restrictions.
Marking and Cutting	▪ except for recreation or aesthetic purposes, no marking will be done within a minimum of 30 metres (98.5 feet) (slope dependent) of any body of water or associated wetland complex, public road, and railway right-of-way, within 60 metres (197 feet) of portages and MNR-authorized trails, or within 15 metres (49 feet) of the Algonquin Park boundary. ▪ all slash within 120 metres (394 feet) of publicly used waters, public roads, portages, and MNR-authorized trails must have tops removed from the reserve or lopped at a safe level. ▪ harvesting will not occur on islands.
Camps, Other Structures, and Improvements	▪ new logging camps, other than the non-mobile camp at Odenback, will be located out of sight and more than 0.8 kilometres (0.5 miles) from canoe routes, portages, and trails. Only temporary portable work camps are permitted.

APPENDIX G
Operational Guidelines for Class I *Special Management Areas*

The following are the operational guidelines for all Class I Special Management Areas (SMA) identified within Algonquin Park. The purpose of these guidelines is to provide adequate protection for earth science values (features) while allowing the harvest of timber where site conditions and existing zoning permit.

The SMA guidelines will ensure this protection occurs by means of access provisions, modified operations, or reserve status (no operations). Normal operations may be carried out where the earth science resource values will not be diminished.

"Core" areas will be protected from any aggregate removal, road building, and site preparation.

The general operational guidelines for the main body of the SMA will be discussed first, followed by the more specific guidelines needed to protect core features.

General Operational Guidelines for Special Management Areas

i) No aggregate extraction: where the size of the SMA exceeds 1 620 hectares (4 000 acres), aggregate removal areas may be designated after the impact on the landform has been assessed. This will allow gravel extraction in three SMAs — 19, 26, and 27 — whose size would create hauling constraints. All other SMAs have gravel adjacent to their boundaries. No material from within an SMA is to be used for projects outside that particular SMA. No "core" area is to be designated for aggregate removal. Extraction areas are to be located outside core areas (it is more desirable to utilize a flat-lying outwash deposit or ground moraine as opposed to a small kame or esker).

ii) No additional primary roads; maintain the route of present existing primary roads.

iii) Secondary roads may be built **only** where timber is otherwise **inaccessible**.

iv) Locate tertiary roads and skid trials so as to minimize the impact on the landscape; avoid small features (DeGeer Moraines, fluvial terraces).

v) Minimize the number of new landings, as these are areas of intense site disturbance. No landings in "core" areas. Where possible utilize existing landings **except** in "core" areas.

vi) Minimal road allowances, except where erosion will result from unstable slopes or **safety** is at issue. All material should be graded to their natural angle of repose as this is the only slope at which materials will be stable. These guidelines govern aggregate and access provisions. Forest management practices should be close to "normal" within much of the larger SMAs. However, for the "core" areas that contain the more sensitive or significant features, more stringent guidelines are necessary to protect these values.

Specific Guidelines for Core Areas

i) No primary, secondary, or tertiary roads; **existing** roads will be accommodated by means of a boundary easement.

ii) No aggregate extraction, including wayside pits.

iii) No clear-cutting, regardless of the species present.

iv) No landings; necessary landings will be located outside core areas.

v) No mechanical site preparation.

Timber harvesting will be permitted only where all of the above restrictions have been met and site conditions permit. These core areas should be carefully monitored during operations. If problems such as gullying, wind erosion, or excessive surface disturbance are evident, the operations should cease. If a core area is affected, then the cause and results should be **documented**. It may be necessary to afford the site a higher degree of protection by designating the affected core area as a **reserve** within the SMA.

The following areas have been identified as Class 1 Special Management Areas with identification numbering after Spek (1993):

I.D. No.	SMA Name	Area (ha.)
16	Petwawa River Terraces	318
17	Sunfish Lake Moraine	91
18	Grosbeak Creek Outwash	546
19	North Rouge Creek Drumlins	1697
20	**Grassy Bay Kame Complex**	**737**
21	Radiant Lake Kame Terraces	508
22	Proulx Lake Outwash	492
23	Modern Fluvial Deltas (3)	69
24	Grand Lake Boulder Pavement	42
25	Achray Beaches/Deposits	37
26	**Lake Travers Outwash Plain**	**7416**
27	**White Partridge Lake Spillway**	**3185**
28	Notsolong Lake Esker	299
29	Hogan Lake Esker	225

GLOSSARY

Allowable cut — The amount of forest produce, however measured, that can be cut in a given period under sustained yield management.

Annual Work Schedule — A statement, mainly in tabular form, showing the order and extent of all work of any nature to be carried out during one year, consistent with the Forest Management Plan.

Baitfish — Any fish that are legally harvested by the commercial bait fish industry.

Carrying capacity — The amount of goods and services that a site can support and sustain without deterioration.

Calcicolous — A plant normally growing on calcareous (lime-rich) soils.

Clear-cut system — An even-aged silvicultural system where the entire growth is harvested over a variable area in one operation, with or without leaving seed-trees.

COSSARIO — Committee on the Status of Species at Risk in Ontario is a committee of representatives from the Ministry of Natural Resources and private agencies that assigns provincial status on species at risk in Ontario.

COSEWIC — Committee on the Status of Endangered Wildlife in Canada is a committee of representatives from federal, provincial and territorial governments, and private agencies that assigns national status to species at risk in Canada.

Endangered — Any native species that, on the basis of the best available scientific evidence, is at risk of extinction or extirpation throughout all or a significant portion of its Ontario range if the limiting factors are not reversed.

Forest Management Plan — A written document containing pertinent information and prescriptions by means of which forest policy, aims and objectives are translated into a continuity of specific treatments on a forest estate for a specified period of years.

Hand cart — A conveyance (portable or otherwise) on wheels, which is pulled by human muscle-power and used for the transport and movement of supplies over a portage.

Mast-producing tree — A tree producing nuts (e.g., acorns or beechnuts) that serve as food for a variety of animals.

Non-productive forest land — That part of the forest ecosystem that consists of treed muskeg, open muskeg, rock, and bush and alder.

Old growth red and white pine forest — Old growth forest ecosystems characterized by the presence of old trees and their associated plants, animals and ecological processes showing little or no evidence of human disturbance. Structural traits include but are not limited to snags, trees with dead or dying tops, downed logs in varying stages of decay, a multi-layered canopy and (for red and white pine) trees 121 years of age and older.

Patch-cutting — A type of clear-cutting in which the cut area may be as small as 1 hectare in size.

Personal electronic device — A radio, cassette player or similar listening device that is incapable of emitting audible sounds without headphones and includes two-way radios.

Primary roads — Constructed, maintained and used as the main all-weather road system providing access to Crown land for a variety of uses. They are essentially permanent roads with an expected life in excess of 15 years.

Recreation Opportunity — A measure of recreation supply that is used to describe the number of times a resource or facility can be used in a given time period. An opportunity is considered not to be greater than one day.

Secondary roads — Designed for use as all-weather roads and are essentially branches of primary roads, providing access to Crown land with an expected life of 5 to 15 years.

Selection system — An uneven-aged silvicultural system where mature and/or undesirable trees, individually or in small groups, are removed over the whole area, usually in the course of a cutting cycle.

Shelterwood — An even-aged silvicultural system system where mature trees are harvested in a series of two or more cuts for the purpose of obtaining natural regeneration under the shelter of the residual trees, whether by cutting uniformly over the entire stand area or in narrow strips.

Sportfish — Any fish that are legally caught by angling.

Sustainable forestry — The practice of forest management that ensures the long-term health of forest ecosystems and that contributes to global environmental benefits while providing an array of social, cultural and economic opportunities now and in the future.

Sustained yield — Production of a biological resource under management procedures that ensure replacement of the part harvested by regrowth or reproduction before another harvest occurs.

Tertiary roads — Constructed to provide for short-term use (up to 5 years) and usually used to provide access for annual harvest and subsequent renewal activities, and becoming reforested over time.

Threatened — Any native species that, on the basis of the best available scientific evidence, is at risk of becoming endangered throughout all or a significant portion of its Ontario range if the limiting factors are not reversed.

Tolerant — The relative capacity of a forest plant to survive and thrive in the understorey (shade). A forest tree that can survive and prosper under a forest canopy is said to be *tolerant* while one that can thrive only in the main canopy or in the open (in the sun) is classified as *intolerant*.

Viable population — A population that, through natural reproduction, is maintaining or expanding its numbers.

Vulnerable — Any native species hat, on the basis of the best available scientific evidence, is a species of special concern in Ontario, but is not a threatened or endangered species.

Wetland — Lands that are seasonally or permanently covered with shallow water, as well as lands where the water table is close to or at the surface. In either case the presence of abundant water has caused the formation of hydric soils and has favoured the dominance of either hydrophytic or water-tolerant plants.

REFERENCES

Allester, David. "Algonquin Region Historical Systems Study." Unpublished report, Ontario Ministry of Natural Resources, Algonquin Region, Huntsville, 1980.

Algonquin Forestry Authority. Algonquin Provincial Park Forest Management Plan. Huntsville, 1995-2015.

Brunton, D. F. Life Science Areas of Natural and Scientific Interest in Site District 5-9. Huntsville: Ontario Ministry of Natural Resources, Algonquin Region, 1991.

__________. Life Science Areas of Natural and Scientific Interest in Site District 5-10. Huntsville: Ontario Ministry of Natural Resources, Algonquin Region, 1991.

Crins, W. J. "Algonquin Provincial Park — Life Science Nature Reserve Zone System Boundary Determination Guidelines and Notes." Unpublished report. Ontario Ministry of Natural Resources, Algonquin Region, Huntsville, 1992.

Davidson, R.J. "A Research and Information Strategy Part One: Setting Priorities." Occasional Paper Number 2, Ontario Parks, Planning and Research Section, Peterborough, 1997.

Friends of Algonquin Park. *The Raven* (newsletter). Whitney, 1985-1997.

Ontario. Department of Lands and Forests. Algonquin Park Task Force: Interim Guidelines for Planning and Management. Queen's Printer, Toronto, 1970.

Ontario. Ministry of Environment. Environmental Guidelines for Access Roads and Water Crossings. Queen's Printer, Toronto, 1988.

Ontario. Ministry of Natural Resources. A Framework for the Conservation of Ontario's Biological Heritage. Parks and Recreational Areas Branch, Toronto, 1980.

__________. A Framework for the Conservation of Ontario's Earth Science Features. Parks and Recreational Areas Branch, Toronto, 1981.

__________. Algonquin Park Fisheries Management Plan 1986-2000. Whitney, 1986.

__________. Algonquin Provincial Park Advisory Committee Report: Government Policy. Queen's Printer, Toronto, 1973.

__________. Algonquin Provincial Park East Side Wilderness Study, Whitney, 1993.

__________. Algonquin Provincial Park Master Plan. Queen's Printer, Toronto, 1974.

__________. Algonquin Provincial Park Master Plan Review 1989-90. Queen's Printer, Toronto, 1991.

__________. Code of Practice for Timber Management Operations in Riparian Areas. Queen's Printer, Toronto, 1991.

__________. Aggregate Resources in Provincial Parks. Ontario Parks, 'Draft' Policy P.M. 11.03.03. Toronto, 1993.

__________. Forest Management Guidelines for the Protection of Cultural Heritage Resources. Queen's Printer, Toronto, 1991.

__________. Lands for Life: A Commitment to the Future. Queen's Printer, Toronto, 1997.

__________. Nature's Best — Ontario's Parks and Protected Areas: A Framework and Action Plan. Queen's Printer, Toronto, 1997.

__________. Ontario Prescribed Burn Planning Manual. Queen's Printer, Toronto, 1988.

__________. Ontario Provincial Park Operating Standards. Queen's Printer, Toronto, 1992.

__________. Ontario Provincial Parks Planning and Management Policies. Queen's Printer, Toronto, 1978, rev. 1992.

__________. "Research Activities in Provincial Parks." Ontario Parks, Policy P.M. 2.45. Toronto, 1994.

__________. Rules and Regulations for Hunting: Algonquin Provincial Park. Whitney, 1997.

__________. The Provincial Parks Council Fifth Annual Report: Algonquin Provincial Park First Five-Year Review 1978-79. Toronto, 1979.

__________. Timber Management Guidelines for the Protection of Fish Habitat.. Queen's Printer, Toronto, 1988.

__________. Timber Management Guidelines for the Protection of Tourism Values. Queen's Printer, Toronto, 1986.

__________. Timber Management Guidelines for the Provision of Moose Habitat.. Queen's Printer, Toronto, 1988.

Spek, C. M. Protecting and Managing Significant Glacial Landforms in Algonquin Provincial Park with Emphasis on Nature Reserve Zones and Areas of Concern: Open File Earth Science Report 9301. Huntsville: Ontario Ministry of Natural Resources, Central Region, 1993.

__________. Regional Earth Science Systems Plan. Huntsville: Ontario Ministry of Natural Resources, Algonquin Region, 1990.

Strickland et al. "Algonquin Provincial Park Visitor Services Plan." Unpublished report, Ontario Ministry of Natural Resources, Whitney, 1981.

INDEX